THOUSAND YEARS OF ENGLISH POETRY

— *Edited by Andrew Pagett* —

CHAUCER PRESS
LONDON

Published by Chaucer Press
an imprint of the Caxton Publishing Group
20 Bloomsbury Street
London WC1B 3JH

© Chaucer Press, 2003

ISBN 1 904449 08 5

Designed and produced for Chaucer Press
by Savitri Books Ltd

WATCHING THE SCOTS GUARDS FROM MARLBOROUGH HOUSE IN LONDON

CONTENTS

TRADITIONAL DORSET COTTAGE

INTRODUCTION

A collection spanning a thousand years covers the lifetime of poetry in English. The earliest poems included here contain many unfamiliar words, and anything before the eighteenth century has, to modern eyes, only a haphazard idea of spelling. By the time Dr Johnson's dictionary had standardised this, purists had also established rules to which all works of art should conform – rules that artists of every discipline have deliberately been breaking ever since.

The result is a body of work of breathtaking diversity. When we consider that the poets included here chose subjects as varied as the birth of the United States, the evils of modern architecture and the stubbornness of an unco-operative tractor, we begin to realise just how broad the canvas is.

There are, nevertheless, recurring themes. God, life and death, love – requited or unrequited – and the natural world have probably inspired poets more often than any other subjects, but the treatments are so varied that almost all the poems in this collection still seem as fresh as they must have done when they were written. Herrick and Marvell urging their lady-loves to stop wasting precious time on maidenly virtue make us smile today as they would have done

four hundred years ago; Oscar Wilde lamenting a relationship that has ended in bitterness can equally make us weep. Gerard Manley Hopkins chooses to thank God for dappled things, while Shelley evokes the heavenly qualities of the skylark and Ted Hughes praises the resilience of the thistle. Even the First World War poets, united in their tragedy, offer the contrast between Rupert Brooke's poignant homesickness for

Grantchester and Wilfred Owen's bitterness at men dying like cattle.

And then there are the oddities – William Oldys' address to a fly drinking out of his cup; Samuel Taylor Coleridge waking from an opium-induced dream to write about Kubla Khan and his 'stately pleasure dome' at Xanadu; Frances Cornford speculating on the sad life of an unknown fat lady seen from a train.

English poetry was, of course, born in England, but sailed the Atlantic with the Pilgrim Fathers, and the two cultures have been cross-fertilising each other ever since. The earliest American poet, Anne Bradstreet, may not be widely read outside the United States, but many others, including Walt Whitman, Robert Frost, Emily Dickinson and T. S. Eliot, are rightly admired throughout the English-speaking world.

The length of the poems varies so enormously that it is pointless to draw conclusions or attempt to make judgements. It is a matter of individual preference whether one is awestruck by the vast sweep of Spenser's epic 'Faerie Queene' or Coleridge's 'Ancient Mariner', or impressed by the fact that Shakespeare could often say all he needed to say within the fourteen lines permitted by a sonnet. (Though we can, of course, choose to admire both.)

So do these poems have anything in common, other than the fact that they were written in English? Perhaps not. Most of them rhyme. Most of them follow a recognisable metric pattern. But these qualities are surely of less importance than the sheer beauty of language – or, perhaps, the sheer *appropriateness* of language when the subject is a harsh or commonplace one – which characterises them all. English has the richest vocabulary of any language in the western world, and the poets in this collection have taken full advantage of that fact. All human life – and much more – is here, and it is depicted by some of the most talented writers ever to put pen to paper or finger to keyboard.

This collection begins with one of the earliest known English lyrics,
dating at the latest from the first half of the thirteenth century.
It is a simple, cheerful hymn to nature.

CUCKOO SONG

Sumer is icumen in,
Loude sing, cuckoo!
Groweth seed and bloweth meed
And spring'th the woode now –
Sing cuckoo!

Ewe bleateth after lamb,
Low'th after calfe cow;
Bullock starteth, bucke farteth.
Merry sing, cuckoo!

Cuckoo, Cuckoo!
Well sing'st thou, cuckoo:
Ne swike thou never now!

Sing cuckoo, now! Sing, cuckoo!
Sing cuckoo! Sing, cuckoo, now!

OPPOSITE. SPRING TASKS IN THE FIELDS

ENGLISH POETRY

WILLIAM LANGLAND (C. 1330-1386)

Little is known of the life of this earliest of English poets, though he seems to have been born in Ledbury (in modern Herefordshire) and spent much of his later life in London. 'Piers Plowman' is the only one of his works that has come down to us. It is the best surviving example of the 'Alliterative Revival' of the mid fourteenth-century, when English poetry reverted to the device of alliteration (repetition of the same initial letter, as in 'somer seson soft sunne' in the first line), which had been common in Old English up to the eleventh century.
In the intervening three hundred years, English poetry had tended to follow the continental model of verse based on rhyme and regular metre, so 'Piers Plowman' has the additional interest of striking a blow for a long-lost English tradition.

PIERS PLOWMAN (extract)

In a somer seson whan soft was the sunne
I shope me in shroudes as I a sheepe were;
In habite as an heremite unholy of workes
Went wide in this world wondres to here.
Ac on a May morninge on Malverne hilles
Me bifel a ferly, of fairy me thoughte.
I was wery forwandred and went me to reste
Under a brode banke bi a burnes side,
And as I lay and lened and loked in the wateres,
I slombred in a slceping, it sweyved so merie.
Thanne gan I to meten a merveilouse swevene,
That I was in a wilderncsse, wist I never where.
As I bihelde into the est, an hiegh to the sunne,
I seigh a toure on a toft trielich ymaked;

A depe dale binethe, a dongeon thereinne
With depe diches and derke and dredful of sight.
A faire felde ful of folke fonde I there bitwene,
Of alle maner of mecn, the mene and the riche,
Worching and wandring as the worlde asketh.
Some putten hem to the plow, pleyed ful selde,
In setting and in sowing swonken ful harde,
And wonnen that wastours with glotonye destruveth.
And some putten hem to pruyde, apparailed hem thereafter,
In contenaunce of clothing comen disgised.

GEOFFREY CHAUCER (1343?-1400)

If Langland is the great poet of the Middle English period, Chaucer – though only a handful of years his junior – may be considered the father of modern English poetry. His greatest work, 'The Canterbury Tales', runs to 17,000 lines of verse and prose, though it is mostly written in rhyming couplets, which were easy to memorise at a time when widespread illiteracy made the oral tradition of particular importance. In the opening section, from which these extracts are taken, the poet describes how he came to meet the twenty-nine 'sondry folk' who were about to embark on a pilgrimage to Canterbury, and describes the looks and personalities of each.

PROLOGUE TO THE CANTERBURY TALES (extracts)

Bifel that, in that seson on a day,
In Southwerk at the Tabard as I lay
Redy to wenden on my pilgrimage

To Caunterbury with ful devout corage,

At night was come into that hostelrye

Wel nine and twenty in a companye,

Of sondry folk, by aventure yfalle

In felawshipe, and pilgrims were they alle,

That toward Caunterbury wolden ride;

The chambres and the stables weren wide,

And wel we weren esed atte beste.

And shortly, whan the sonne was to reste,

So hadde I spoken with hem everichon,

That I was of hir felawshipe anon,

And made forward erly for to rise,

To take our wey, ther as I yow devise.

But natheles, whil I have time and space,

Er that I ferther in this tale pace,

Me thinketh it acordaunt to resoun,

To telle yow al the condicioun

Of ech of hem, so as it semed me,

And whiche they weren, and of what degree

And eek in what array that they were inne

And at a knight than wol I first biginne.

A Knight ther was, and that a worthy man,

That fro the time that he first bigan

To riden out, he loved chivalrye,

Trouthe and honour, freedom and curteisye.

Ful worthy was he in his lordes werre,

And therto hadde he ridden, no man ferre,

As wel in Cristendom as hethenesse,

And ever honoured for his worthinesse.

There was also a nun, a Prioress,

That of her smiling was full simple and coy;

Her greatest oath was but by Saint Loy;

And she was clepèd Madam Eglantine.

Full well she sang the service divine,

Entuned in her nose full seemely,

And French she spake full fair and fetisly,

After the school of Stratford-atte-Bow,

For French of Paris was to her unknow.

At meate well y-taught was she withal;

She let no morsel from her lippes fall,

Ne wet her fingers in her sauce deep;

Well could she carry a morsel and well keep

That no droppe ne fell upon her breast.

In courtesy was set full much her lest.

Her over-lippe wipèd she so clean

That in her cup there was no farthing seen

Of grease, when she drunken had her draught.

Full seemely after her meat she raught.

And sikerly she was of great desport,

And full pleasant, and amiable of port,

And peynèd her to counterfeite cheer

Of court, and been estately of manner

And to ben holden digne of reverence.

But, for to speaken of her conscience,

She was so charitable and so piteous

She woulde weep, if that she saw a mouse

Caught in a trap, if it were dead or bled.

Of smalle houndes had she that she fed

With roasted flesh, or milk and wastel-bread.

But sore wept she if one of them were dead,

Or if men smote it with a yarde smart;

And all was conscience and tender heart.

Full seemely her wimple pinchèd was;

Her nose tretys, her eyen grey as glass,

Her mouth full small, and thereto soft and red;

But sikerly she had a fair forehead;

It was almost a spanne broad, I trow;

For, hardily, she was not undergrow.

Full fetis was her cloak, as I was ware.

Of small coral about her arm she bore

A pair of beades, gauded all with green,

And thereon hung a brooch of gold full sheen,

On which there was first writ a crownèd 'A',

And after *Amor vincit omnia.*

Another anonymous verse, this one from the mid-fifteenth century. It is interesting to note that although the spelling is still erratic by modern standards, the vocabulary is becoming familiar.

THE MONTHS

Januar: By this fire I warme my handis,

Februar: And with my spade I delfe my landis.

Marche: Here I sette my thinge to springe,

Aprile: And here I heer the fowlis singe.

Maii: I am as light as birde in bowe,

HARVESTING THE GRAPES IN SEPTEMBER

Junii: And I weede my corne well ynow.

Julii: With my sithe my mede I mowe,

Auguste: And here I shere my corne full lowe.

September: With my flaill I erne my brede,

October: And here I sowe my whete so redde.

November: At Martinesmasse I kille my swine

December: And at Cristesmasse I drinke redde wine.

EDMUND SPENSER (1552?-1599)

A strong desire to please their powerful queen influenced the writing of many Elizabethan poets. The title of Spenser's great work The Faerie Queene, *refers specifically to her, as well as to the abstract concept of Glory. In this poem, too, Spenser coined the term 'Gloriana', still often applied to Elizabeth I.*

THE FAERIE QUEENE (extract)

Eftsoones they heard a most melodious sound,

Of all that mote delight a daintie eare,

Such as attonce might not on living ground,

Save in this Paradise, be heard elsewhere:

Right hard it was, for wight which did it heare,

To read what manner musicke that mote bee:

For all that pleasing is to living eare,

Was there consortèd in one harmonee,

Birdes, voyces, instruments, windes, waters, all agree.

The joyous birdes shrouded in chearefull shade,
Their notes unto the voyce attempred sweet;
Th'Angelicall soft trembling voyces made
To th'instruments divine respondence meet:
The silver sounding instruments did meet
With the base murmure of the waters fall:
The waters fall with difference discreet,
Now soft, now loud, unto the wind did call:
The gentle warbling wind low answerèd to all.

There, whence that Musick seemèd heard to bee,
Was the faire Witch her selfe now solacing,
With a new Lover, whom through sorceree
And witchcraft she from farre did thither bring:
There she had him now layd a slombering,
In secret shade, after long wanton joyes:
Whilst round about them pleasauntly did sing
Many faire Ladies, and lascivious boyes,
That ever mixt their song with light licentious toyes.

And all that while, right over him she hung
With her false eyes fast fixèd in his sight,
As seeking medicine, whence she was stung,
Or greedily depasturing delight:
And oft inclining downe with kisses light,
For feare of waking him, his lips bedewd,
And through his humid eyes did sucke his spright,
Quite molten into lust and pleasure lewd;
Wherewith she sighèd soft, as if his case she rewd.

The whiles some one did chaunt this lovely lay;

'Ah see, who so faire thing doest faine to see,

In springing flowre the image of thy day;

Ah see the Virgin Rose, how sweetly shee

Doth first peepe forth with bashful modestee,

That fairer seemes, the lesse ye see her may;

Lo, see soone after how more bold and free

Her barèd bosome she doth broad display;

Lo, see soone after how she fades and falls away.

'So passeth, in the passing of a day,

Of mortall life the leafe, the bud, the flowre,

Ne more doth flourish after first decay,

That earst was sought to decke both bed and bowre,

Of many a Ladie, and many a Paramowre:

Gather therefore the Rose, whilst yet is prime,

For soone comes age, that will her pride deflowre:

Gather the Rose of love, whilst yet is time,

Whilst loving thou mayst lovèd be with equall crime.'

WILLIAM SHAKESPEARE (1564-1616)

In addition to thirty-seven plays, Shakespeare wrote two long poems, 'Venus and Adonis' and 'The Rape of Lucrece'; a number of shorter poems; and 150 sonnets, whose concluding rhyming couplet is characteristic of what became known as the Shakespearian sonnet form. He also included many short songs in his plays – love songs both happy and sorrowful, 'incidental' songs performed during a lull in the action and, as in the case of 'Ariel's Song', cheerful ditties identified with individual characters.

SONNET 29

When, in disgrace with fortune and men's eyes,
I all alone beweep my outcast state,
And trouble deaf heaven with my bootless cries,
And look upon myself, and curse my fate,
Wishing me like to one more rich in hope,
Featured like him, like him with friends possessed,
Desiring this man's art and that man's scope,
With what I most enjoy contented least;
Yet in these thoughts myself almost despising,
Haply I think on thee, and then my state,
Like to the lark at break of day arising
From sullen earth, sings hymns at heaven's gate;
For thy sweet love remembered such wealth brings
That then I scorn to change my state with kings.

SONNET 104

To me, fair friend, you never can be old;
For as you were when first your eye I eyed,
Such seems your beauty still. Three Winters cold
Have from the forests shook three Summers' pride;
Three beauteous Springs to yellow Autumn turn'd
In process of the seasons have I seen,
Three April perfumes in three hot Junes burn'd,
Since first I saw you fresh, which yet are green,
Ah! yet doth beauty, like a dial-hand,
Steal from his figure, and no pace perceived;

So your sweet hue, which methinks still doth stand,

Hath motion, and mine eye may be deceived:

For fear of which, hear this, thou age unbred:

Ere you were born was beauty's Summer dead.

DIRGE (from *Twelfth Night*)

Come away, come away, death,

And in sad cypres let me be laid;

Fly away, fly away, breath;

I am slain by a fair cruel maid.

My shroud of white, stuck all with yew,

O prepare it!

My part of death, no one so true

Did share it.

Not a flower, not a flower sweet,

On my black coffin let there be strown;

Not a friend, not a friend greet

My poor corse, where my bones shall be thrown

A thousand thousand sighs to save,

Lay me, O, where

Sad true lover never find my grave

To weep there!

OPPOSITE. IN THE LEAFY MONTH OF JUNE BY CHARLES DAVIDSON

ARIEL'S SONG (from *The Tempest*)

Where the bee sucks, there suck I:
In a cowslip's bell I lie;
There I couch when owls do cry.
On the bat's back I do fly
After summer merrily:
Merrily, merrily, shall I live now,
Under the blossom that hangs on the bough.

JOHN DONNE (1572-1631)

Donne became famous later in life for his sermons and religious poetry, but as a young man he wrote a collection of passionate and erotic poems under the title Songs and Sonets. *These two poems show how his preoccupations changed as he grew older.*

SONG

Go and catch a falling star,

Get with child a mandrake root,

Tell me where all past years are,

Or who cleft the Devil's foot;

Teach me to hear mermaids singing,

Or to keep off envy's stinging,

And find

What wind

Serves to advance an honest mind.

If thou beest born to strange sights,

Things invisible to see,

Ride ten thousand days and nights

Till Age snow white hairs on thee;

Thou, when thou return'st, wilt tell me

All strange wonders that befell thee,

And swear

No where

Lives a woman true and fair.

If thou find'st one, let me know;

Such a pilgrimage were sweet.

Yet do not; I would not go,

Though at next door we might meet.

Though she were true when you met her,

And last till you write your letter,

Yet she

Will be

False, ere I come, to two or three.

HOLY SONNETS (extract)

Thou hast made me, and shall thy work decay?

Repair me now, for now mine end doth haste;

I run to death, and death meets me as fast,

And all my pleasures are like yesterday.

I dare not move my dim eyes any way;

Despair behind, and death before doth cast

Such terror, and my feebled flesh doth waste

By sin in it, which it towards hell doth weigh.

Only thou art above, and when towards thee

By thy leave I can look, I rise again;

But our old subtle foe so tempteth me

That not one hour I can myself sustain.

Thy grace may wing me to prevent his art,

And thou like adamant draw mine iron heart.

૬ૐૐ

Members of the religious group known as the Puritans played a powerful role in British politics in the seventeenth century. Persecution by the established church led Puritans to leave the country in 1620, setting sail on the Mayflower *to found a colony in the New World. Only ten years later, Anne Bradstreet, known as the first American poet, followed them with her husband, who became Governor of Massachusetts. Back in England, Milton's total submission to the will of God is typical of the Puritan ethic.*

JOHN MILTON (1608-1674)

ON HIS BLINDNESS

When I consider how my light is spent,
Ere half my days, in this dark world and wide,
And that one Talent which is death to hide,
Lodg'd with me useless, though my Soul more bent
To serve therewith my Maker, and present
My true account, least he returning chide,
Doth God exact day-labour, light deny'd,
I fondly ask; But patience to prevent
That murmur, soon replies, God doth not need
Either man's work or his own gifts, who best
Bear his milde yoak, they serve him best, his State
Is Kingly. Thousands at his bidding speed
And post o're Land and Ocean without rest:
They also serve who only stand and wait.

On Time

Fly envious Time, till thou run out thy race,
Call on the lazy leaden-stepping hours,
Whose speed is but the heavy Plummets pace;
And glut thy self with what thy womb devours,
Which is no more then what is false and vain,
And meerly mortal dross;
So little is our loss,
So little is thy gain.
For when as each thing bad thou hast entomb'd,
And last of all, thy greedy self consum'd,
Then long Eternity shall greet our bliss
With an individual kiss;
And Joy shall overtake us as a flood,
When every thing that is sincerely good
And perfectly divine,
With Truth, and Peace, and Love shall ever shine
About the supreme Throne
Of him, t'whose happy-making sight alone,
When once our heav'nly-guidèd soul shall clime,
Then all this Earthy grosnes quit,
Attir'd with Stars, we shall for ever sit,
Triumphing over Death, and Chance, and thee O Time.

ANNE BRADSTREET (1612-1672)

Anne Bradstreet's first poems were published in London without her knowledge, and although they were flatteringly entitled 'The Tenth Muse Lately Sprung Up in America', this poem may reflect the author's embarrassment.

THE AUTHOR TO HER BOOK

Thou ill-form'd offspring of my feeble brain,
Who after birth did'st by my side remain,
Till snatcht from thence by friends, less wise than true
Who thee abroad expos'd to publick view,
Made thee in raggs, halting to th' press to trudg,
Where errors were not lessened (all may judg).
At thy return my blushing was not small,
My rambling brat (in print) should mother call,
I cast thee by as one unfit for light,
Thy Visage was so irksome in my sight;
Yet being mine own, at length affection would
Thy blemishes amend, if so l could:
I wash'd thy face, but more defects I saw
And rubbing off a spot, still made a flaw.
I stretcht thy joynts to make thee even feet,
Yet still thou run'st more hobling then is meet;
In better dress to trim thee was my mind,
But nought save home-spun Cloth, i'th' house I find
In this array, 'mongst Vulgars mayst thou roam
In Criticks hands, beware thou dost not come;
And take thy way where yet thou art not known,

If for thy Father askt, say, thou hadst none:

And for thy Mother, she alas is poor,

Which caus'd her thus to send thee out of door.

Educated people of the seventeenth century were well versed in the Classics, and the Latin poet Horace's famous advice to 'seize the day' would have been familiar to Herrick, Marvell and their contemporaries. They frequently translated this dictum into a warning that old age and death were approaching all too quickly. These two sprightly poems are urgent pleas from a young man to the object of his affections not to waste time in maidenly restraint when it could be better spent in love making.

ROBERT HERRICK (1591-1674)

TO THE VIRGINS, TO MAKE MUCH OF TIME

Gather ye rosebuds while ye may,

Old Time is still a-flying:

And this same flower that smiles to-day

To-morrow will be dying.

The glorious lamp of heaven, the sun,

The higher he's a-getting,

The sooner will his race be run,

And nearer he's to setting.

That age is best which is the first,

When youth and blood are warmer;

But being spent, the worse, and worst
Times still succeed the former.

Then be not coy, but use your time,
And while ye may, go marry:
For having lost but once your prime,
You may for ever tarry.

ANDREW MARVELL (1621-1678)

TO HIS COY MISTRESS

Had we but world enough, and time,
This coyness, Lady, were no crime.
We would sit down, and think which way
To walk, and pass our long love's day.
Thou by the Indian Ganges' side
Shouldst rubies find: I by the tide
Of Humber would complain. I would
Love you ten years before the Flood:
And you should, if you please, refuse
Till the conversion of the Jews.
My vegetable love should grow
Vaster than empires, and more slow.
An hundred years should go to praise
Thine eyes, and on thy forehead gaze.
Two hundred to adore each breast:
But thirty thousand to the rest.
An age at least to every part,

And the last age should show your heart.

For, Lady, you deserve this state;

Nor would I love at lower rate.

But at my back I always hear

Time's wingèd chariot hurrying near

And yonder all before us lie

Deserts of vast eternity.

Thy beauty shall no more be found;

Nor, in thy marble vault, shall sound

My echoing song; then worms shall try

That long preserved virginity:

And your quaint honour turn to dust;

And into ashes all my lust.

The grave's a fine and private place,

But none I think do there embrace.

Now therefore, while the youthful hue

Sits on thy skin like morning dew,

And while thy willing soul transpires

At every pore with instant fires,

Now let us sport us while we may;

And now, like amorous birds of prey,

Rather at once our time devour,

Than languish in his slow-chapt power.

Let us roll all our strength, and all

Our sweetness, up into one ball:

And tear our pleasures with rough strife,

Through the iron gates of life.

Thus, though we cannot make our sun

Stand still, yet we will make him run.

The period known as the Renaissance refers largely to a rebirth of interest in Classical literature, art and architecture, much of it sparked by the rediscovery of many ancient manuscripts after Constantinople, which had been a great seat of learning, fell to the Turks in 1453 and Christian scholars scattered across Europe. For the next four hundred years, many poets and playwrights deliberately imitated the style of the ancient Romans and Greeks, some even following the strict rules laid down by Aristotle on the proper way of constructing tragedies. Dryden, Swift and Pope were all followers of this Neo-Classical school.

JOHN DRYDEN (1631-1700)

HAPPY THE MAN

Happy the man, and happy he alone,
He who can call today his own:
He who, secure within, can say,
Tomorrow do thy worst, for I have lived today.
Be fair or foul or rain or shine
The joys I have possessed, in spite of fate, are mine.
Not Heaven itself upon the past has power,
But what has been, has been, and I have had my hour.

JONATHAN SWIFT (1667-1745)

WRITTEN IN A LADY'S IVORY TABLE-BOOK 1698

Peruse my leaves thro' ev'ry part,
And think thou seest my owner's heart,

Scrawl'd o'er with trifles thus, and quite

As hard, as senseless, and as light;

Expos'd to ev'ry coxcomb's eyes,

But hid with caution from the wise.

Here you may read, 'Dear charming saint';

Beneath, 'A new receipt for paint':

Here, in beau-spelling, 'Tru tel deth';

There, in her own, 'For an el breth':

Here, 'Lovely nymph, pronounce my doom!'

There, 'A safe way to use perfume':

Here, a page fill'd with billets-doux;

THE BISHOP'S PALACE IN WELLS BY WALTER TYNDALE

On t'other side, 'Laid out for shoes'

'Madam, I die without your grace'

'Item, for half a yard of lace.'

Who that had wit would place it here,

For every peeping fop to jeer ?

In pow'r of spittle and a clout,

Whene'er he please, to blot it out;

And then, to heighten the disgrace,

Clap his own nonsense in the place.

Whoe'er expects to hold his part

In such a book, and such a heart,

If he be wealthy, and a fool,

Is in all points the fittest tool;

Of whom it may be justly said,

He's a gold pencil tipp'd with lead.

ALEXANDER POPE (1688-1744)

OF THE NATURE AND STATE OF MAN WITH RESPECT TO HIMSELF, AS AN INDIVIDUAL

(from *An Essay on Man*)

Know then thyself, presume not God to scan;

The proper study of mankind is Man.

Placed on this isthmus of a middle state,

A being darkly wise, and rudely great:

With too much knowledge for the skeptic side,

With too much weakness for the Stoic's pride,

He hangs between; in doubt to act, or rest,

In doubt to deem himself a god, or beast;

In doubt his mind or body to prefer,

Born but to die, and reasoning but to err,

Alike in ignorance, his reason such,

Whether he thinks too little, or too much:

Chaos of thought and passion, all confused;

Still by himself abused, or disabused;

Created half to rise, and half to fall;

Great lord of all things, yet a prey to all;

Sole judge of truth, in endless error hurled:

The glory, jest, and riddle of the world!

WILLIAM OLDYS (1696-1761)

William Oldys was primarily a historian, biographer and editor, his best known work being a biography of Sir Walter Raleigh, used as an introduction to the 1736 edition of Raleigh's History of the World. *This appealing ditty is the only one of his poems that is now remembered.*

ON A FLY DRINKING OUT OF HIS CUP

Busy, curious, thirsty fly!

Drink with me and drink as I:

Freely welcome to my cup,

Couldst thou sip and sip it up:

Make the most of life you may,

Life is short and wears away.

Both alike are mine and thine
Hastening quick to their decline:
Thine's a summer, mine's no more,
Though repeated to threescore.
Threescore summers, when they're gone,
Will appear as short as one!

Thomas Gray (1716-1771)

Gray's famous 'Elegy' was inspired by the churchyard of Stoke Poges in Buckinghamshire. Its realistic portrayal of nature belongs to the Neo-Classical tradition, but the pure beauty of its language owes nothing to hard and fast rules. It has often been assumed that Gray's concern for some 'mute, inglorious Milton' reflected anxiety about what heed posterity would pay to his own works. He need surely not have worried.

Elegy Written in a Country Churchyard

The curfew tolls the knell of parting day,
The lowing herd wind slowly o'er the lea,
The plowman homeward plods his weary way,
And leaves the world to darkness and to me.

Now fades the glimmering landscape on the sight,
And all the air a solemn stillness holds,
Save where the beetle wheels his droning flight,
And drowsy tinklings lull the distant folds;

Save that from yonder ivy-mantled tower
The moping owl does to the moon complain
Of such as, wand'ring near her secret bower,
Molest her ancient solitary reign.

Beneath those rugged elms, that yew-tree's shade,
Where heaves the turf in many a mould'ring heap,
Each in his narrow cell for ever laid,
The rude forefathers of the hamlet sleep.

The breezy call of incense-breaking morn,
The swallow twitt'ring from the straw-built shed,
The cock's shrill clarion, or the echoing horn,
No more shall rouse them from their lowly bed.

For them no more the blazing hearth shall burn,
Or busy housewife ply her evening care:
No children run to lisp their sire's retum,
Or climb his knees the envied kiss to share.

Oft did the harvest to their sickle yield,
Their furrow oft the stubborn glebe has broke:
How jocund did they drive their team afield!
How bowed the woods beneath their sturdy stroke!

Let not Ambition mock their useful toil,
Their homely joys, and destiny obscure;
Nor Grandeur hear with a disdainful smile
The short and simple annals of the poor.

The boast of heraldry, the pomp of power,
And all that beauty, all that wealth e'er gave,
Awaits alike th' inevitable hour:
The paths of glory lead but to the grave.

Nor you, ye proud, impute to These the fault,
If Memory o'er their tomb no trophies raise,
Where through the long-drawn aisle and fretted vault
The pealing anthem swells the note of praise.

Can storied urn or animated bust
Back to its mansion call the fleeting breath?
Can Honour's voice provoke the silent dust,
Or Flatt'ry soothe the dull cold ear of death?

Perhaps in this neglected spot is laid
Some heart once pregnant with celestial fire;
Hands, that the rod of empire might have swayed,
Or waked to ecstasy the living lyre.

But Knowledge to their eyes her ample page
Rich with the spoils of time did ne'er unroll;
Chill Penury repressed their noble rage,
And froze the genial current of the soul.

Full many a gem of purest ray serene
The dark unfathomed caves of ocean bear:
Full many a flower is born to blush unseen,
And waste its sweetness on the desert air.

CLOISTERS AND FROMOND'S CHANTRY, WINCHESTER COLLEGE

Some village Hampden that with dauntless breast
The little tyrant of his fields withstood,
Some mute inglorious Milton here may rest,
Some Cromwell guiltless of his country's blood.

Th' applause of list'ning senates to command,
The threats of pain and ruin to despise,
To scatter plenty o'er a smiling land,
And read their history in a nation's eyes,

Their lot forbade: nor circumscribed alone
Their growing virtues, but their crimes confined;
Forbade to wade through slaughter to a throne.
And shut the gates of mercy on mankind,

The struggling pangs of conscious truth to hide,
To quench the blushes of ingenuous shame,
Or heap the shrine of luxury and Pride
With incense kindled at the Muse's flame.

Far from the madding crowd's ignoble strife
Their sober wishes never learned to stray;
Along the cool sequestered vale of life
They kept the noiseless tenor of their way.

Yet ev'n these bones from insult to protect
Some frail memorial still erected nigh,
With uncouth rhymes and shapeless sculpture decked,
Implores the passing tribute of a sigh.

Their name, their years, spelt by th'unlettered Muse,
The place of fame and elegy supply:
And many a holy text around she strews,
That teach the rustic moralist to die.

For who, to dumb Forgetfulness a prey,
This pleasing anxious being e'er resigned,
Left the warm precincts of the cheerful day,
Nor cast one longing ling'ring look behind?

On some fond breast the parting soul relies,
Some pious drops the closing eye requires;
E'en from the tomb the voice of Nature cries,
E'en in our Ashes live their wonted fires.

For thee, who, mindful of th'unhonoured dead
Dost in these lines their artless tale relate;
If chance, by lonely contemplation led,
Some kindred spirit shall inquire thy fate,

Haply some hoary-headed Swain may say,
'Oft have we seen him at the peep of dawn
Brushing with hasty steps the dews away
To meet the sun upon the upland lawn.

'There at the foot of yonder nodding beech
That wreathes its old fantastic roots so high,
His listless length at noontide would he stretch,
And pore upon the brook that babbles by.

'Hard by yon wood, now smiling as in scorn,
Mutt'ring his wayward fancies he would rove,
Now drooping, woeful wan, like one forlorn,
Or crazed with care, or crossed in hopeless love.

'One morn I missed him on the customed hill
Along the heath and near his fav'rite tree;
Another came; nor yet beside the rill,
Nor up the lawn, nor at the wood was he;

'The next with dirges due in sad array
Slow through the churchway path we saw him borne.
Approach and read (for thou canst read) the lay
Graved on the stone beneath yon aged thorn:'

The Epitaph

Here rests his head upon the lap of Earth
A Youth to Fortune and to Fame unknown.
Fair Science frowned not on his humble birth,
And Melancholy marked him for her own.

Large was his bounty, and his soul sincere,
Heaven did a recompense as largely send:
He gave to Mis'ry all he had, a tear,
He gained from Heaven ('twas all he wished) a friend.

No further seek his merits to disclose,
Or draw his frailties from their dread abode,
(There they alike in trembling hope repose,)
The bosom of his Father and his God.

FROM THE DEAN'S ORCHARD, MERE, WILTSHIRE

ENGLISH POETRY

OLIVER GOLDSMITH (1730-1774)

*Irish-born Goldsmith had a varied and somewhat ignominious career before he arrived
he achieved a prodigious output of articles, reviews, translations, biographies, histories,
the novel* The Vicar of Wakefield *and a number of plays, including one of
the funniest comedies ever written in English,* She Stoops to Conquer.
*A friend and protégé of Dr Johnson, he was a strong opponent of the vogue for
sentimental comedy and although this verse seems at first glance rather
a lachrymose one, it is surely a satirical gibe at
the double standards of the day.*

SONG

When lovely woman stoops to folly,
And finds too late that men betray,
What charm can sooth her melancholy,
What art can wash her guilt away?

The only art her guilt to cover,
To hide her shame from every eye,
To give repentance to her lover,
And wring his bosom – is to die.

WILLIAM COWPER (1731-1800)

Best known for his long poem John Gilpin, *Cowper was a melancholy character who
turned to evangelical Christianity for consolation and, in collaboration with the
Reverend John Newton, wrote a collection known at the Olney Hymns.*

Not many twenty-first-century readers would describe Cowper as a major poet,
but for all his depression he had a gift for the catchy phrase. The famous first
line of this poem is just one of the expressions he coined that have
passed into the language – 'the worse for wear' and
'variety is the spice of life' are also creations of Cowper's.

LIGHT SHINING OUT OF DARKNESS

God moves in a mysterious way,
His wonders to perform;
He plants his footsteps in the sea,
And rides upon the storm.

Deep in unfathomable mines
Of never failing skill
He treasures up his bright designs,
And works his sovereign will.

Ye fearful saints, fresh courage take,
The clouds ye so much dread
Are big with mercy, and shall break
In blessings on your head.

Judge not the Lord by feeble sense,
But trust him for his grace;
Behind a frowning providence,
He hides a smiling face.

❧❧

His purposes will ripen fast,
Unfolding every hour;
The bud may have a bitter taste,
But sweet will be the flower.

Blind unbelief is sure to err,
And scan his work in vain;
God is his own interpreter,
And he will make it plain.

WILLIAM BLAKE (1757-1827)

His early thinking influenced by the Swedish philospher Swedenborg, Blake believed that human beings, created in God's image, were by their nature divine. He is one of the early poetic rebels, casting off both what he saw as the repressive mantle of conventional Christianity and the emphasis on material things spawned by the philosophical and scientific movement known as the Enlightenment, whose influence spread through the literary world in the eighteenth century. Blake's mysticism is at times a little obscure, but there is no mistaking the power and the beauty of his words.

JERUSALEM

And did those feet in ancient time
Walk upon England's mountains green?
And was the holy lamb of God
On England's pleasant pastures seen?

And did the countenance divine
Shine forth upon our clouded hills?
And was Jerusalem builded here
Among those dark satanic mills?

Bring me my bow of burning gold:
Bring me my arrows of desire:
Bring me my spear: O clouds unfold!
Bring me my chariot of fire.
I will not cease from mental fight,
Nor shall my sword sleep in my hand
Till we have built Jerusalem
In England's green and pleasant land.

The Tyger

Tyger, tyger, burning bright
In the forests of the night,
What immortal hand or eye
Could frame thy fearful symmetry?

In what distant deeps or skies
Burnt the fire of thine eyes?
On what wings dare he aspire?
What the hand dare seize the fire?

And what shoulder and what art
Could twist the sinews of thy heart?

And, when thy heart began to beat,
What dread hand and what dread feet?

What the hammer? What the chain?
In what furnace was thy brain?
What the anvil? What dread grasp
Dare its deadly terrors clasp?

When the stars threw down their spears,
And water'd heaven with their tears,
Did He smile His work to see?
Did He who made the lamb make thee?

Tyger, tyger, burning bright
In the forests of the night,
What immortal hand or eye
Dare frame thy fearful symmetry?

ROBERT BURNS (1759-1796)

Some of Burns' poetry is difficult for anyone born south of the Border to understand. Nevertheless, he ranks as Scotland's greatest poet and has given the world many classics, including 'My love is like a red, red rose', 'The Mouse' ('wee, sleekit, cow'rin', tim'rous beastie'), the blood-curdling 'Address to the Haggis' always recited at Burns Night celebrations – and this, which has become the anthem of New Year's Eve all over the English-speaking world.

AULD LANG SYNE

Should auld acquaintance be forgot,
And never brought to min'?
Should auld acquaintance be forgot,
And auld lang syne?

For auld lang syne, my dear.
For auld lang syne,
We'll tak a cup o' kindness yet,
For auld lang syne.

We twa hae run about the braes,
And pu'd the gowans fine;
But we've wandered mony a weary foot
Sin' auld lang syne.

We twa hae paidled i' the burn,
From morning sun till dine;
But seas between us braid hae roared
Sin' auld lang syne.

And there's a hand, my trusty fiere,
And gie's a hand o' thine;
And we'll tak a right guid-willie waught,
For auld lang syne.

And surely ye'll be your pint-stowp,
And surely I'll be mine;
And we'll tak a cup o' kindness yet
For auld lang syne.

By the end of the eighteenth century, Neo-Classicism was giving way to Romanticism,
a movement which laid emphasis on the value of individual personal experience
and whose writing was characterised by imagination rather than a slavish
desire for realism. The two great 'Lake Poets', Wordsworth and Coleridge,
were early exponents of this style.

WILLIAM WORDSWORTH (1770-1850)

THE DAFFODILS

I wandered lonely as a cloud
That floats on high o'er vales and hills,
When all at once I saw a crowd,
A host, of golden daffodils;
Beside the lake, beneath the trees,
Fluttering and dancing in the breeze.

Continuous as the stars that shine
And twinkle on the milky way,
They stretched in never-ending line
Along the margin of a bay:
Ten thousand saw I at a glance,
Tossing their heads in sprightly dance.

The waves beside them danced; but they
Out-did the sparkling waves in glee:
A poet could not but be gay,
In such a jocund company:
I gazed – and gazed – but little thought
What wealth the show to me had brought:

For oft, when on my couch I lie

In vacant or in pensive mood,

They flash upon that inward eye

Which is the bliss of solitude;

And then my heart with pleasure fills,

And dances with the daffodils.

SONNET COMPOSED UPON WESTMINSTER BRIDGE

SEPTEMBER 3, 1802

Earth has not anything to show more fair:

Dull would he be of soul who could pass by

A sight so touching in its majesty:

This city now doth, like a garment, wear

ALONG THE THAMES EMBANKMENT IN LONDON BY ROSE BARTON

The beauty of the morning; silent, bare,
Ships, towers, domes, theatres, and temples lie
Open unto the fields, and to the sky;
All bright and glittering in the smokeless air.
Never did sun more beautifully steep
In his first splendour, valley, rock, or hill;
Ne'er saw I, never felt, a calm so deep!
The river glideth at his own sweet will:
Dear God! the very houses seem asleep;
And all that mighty heart is lying still!

SAMUEL TAYLOR COLERIDGE (1772-1834)

THE RIME OF THE ANCIENT MARINER (extract)

It is an ancient Mariner
And he stoppeth one of three.
'By thy long grey beard and glittering eye,
Now wherefore stopp'st thou me?

The Bridegroom's doors are opened wide,
And I am next of kin;
The guests are met, the feast is set:
Mayst hear the merry din.'

He holds him with his skinny hand,
'There was a ship,' quoth he.
'Hold off! unhand me, grey-beard loon!'
Eftsoons his hand dropt he.

He holds him with his glittering eye –
The Wedding-Guest stood still,
And listens like a three years' child:
The Mariner hath his will.

The Wedding-Guest sat on a stone:
He cannot choose but hear;
And thus spake on that ancient man,
The bright-eyed Mariner.

'The ship was cheered, the harbour cleared,
Merrily did we drop
Below the kirk, below the hill,
Below the lighthouse top.

The Sun came up upon the left,
Out of the sea came he!
And he shone bright, and on the right
Went down into the sea.

Higher and higher every day,
Till over the mast at noon –'
The Wedding-Guest here beat his breast,
For he heard the loud bassoon.

The bride hath paced into the hall,
Red as a rose is she;
Nodding their heads before her goes
The merry minstrelsy.

The Wedding-Guest he beat his breast,
Yet he cannot choose but hear;
And thus spake on that ancient man,
The bright-eyed Mariner.

'And now the STORM-BLAST came, and he
Was tyrannous and strong:
He struck with his o'ertaking wings,
And chased us south along.

With sloping masts and dipping prow,
As who pursued with yell and blow
Still treads the shadow of his foe,
And forward bends his head,
The ship drove fast, loud roared the blast,
And southward aye we fled.

And now there came both mist and snow,
And it grew wondrous cold:
And ice, mast-high, came floating by,
As green as emerald.

And through the drifts the snowy clifts
Did send a dismal sheen:
Nor shapes of men nor beasts we ken –
The ice was all between.

The ice was here, the ice was there,
The ice was all around:
It cracked and growled, and roared and howled,
Like noises in a swound!

At length did cross an Albatross,
Thorough the fog it came;
As if it had been a Christian soul,
We hailed it in God's name.

It ate the food it ne'er had eat,
And round and round it flew
The ice did split with a thunder-fit;
The helmsman steered us through!

And a good south wind sprung up behind;
The Albatross did follow,
And every day, for food or play,
Came to the mariners' hollo!

In mist or cloud, on mast or shroud,
It perched for vespers nine;
Whiles all the night, through fog-smoke white,
Glimmered the white Moon-shine.'

'God save thee, ancient Mariner!
From the fiends, that plague thee thus!
Why look'st thou so?'- 'With my cross-bow
I shot the ALBATROSS.'

Legend has it that Coleridge dreamed this poem after taking opium to treat a minor illness. On waking, he set about writing it down, but was interrupted by 'a person on business from Porlock'. When he returned to his task, the memory of the dream had vanished.

KUBLA KHAN

OR, A VISION IN A DREAM. A FRAGMENT

In Xanadu did Kubla Khan
A stately pleasure-dome decree:
Where Alph, the sacred river, ran
Through caverns measureless to man
Down to a sunless sea.
So twice five miles of fertile ground
With walls and towers were girded round:
And here were gardens bright with sinuous rills,
Where blossomed many an incense-bearing tree;
And here were forests ancient as the hills,
Enfolding sunny spots of greenery.

But oh! that deep romantic chasm which slanted
Down the green hill athwart a cedarn cover!
A savage place! as holy and enchanted
As e'er beneath a waning moon was haunted
By woman wailing for her demon-lover!
And from this chasm, with ceaseless turmoil seething
As if this earth in fast thick pants were breathing,
A mighty fountain momently was forced:

OPPOSITE. IN THE BAZAAR BY JOHN FREDERICK LEWIS

Amid whose swift half-intermitted burst

Huge fragments vaulted like rebounding hail

Or chaffy grain beneath the thresher's flail:

And 'mid these dancing rocks at once and ever

It flung up momently the sacred river.

Five miles meandering with a mazy motion

Through wood and dale the sacred river ran,

Then reached the caverns measureless to man,

And sank in tumult to a lifeless ocean:

And 'mid this tumult Kubla heard from far

Ancestral voices prophesying war!

The shadow of the dome of pleasure

Floated midway on the waves;

Where was heard the mingled measure

From the fountain and the caves.

It was a miracle of rare device,

A sunny pleasure-dome with caves of ice!

A damsel with a dulcimer

In a vision once I saw:

It was an Abyssinian maid,

And on her dulcimer she played,

Singing of Mount Abora.

Could I revive within me

Her symphony and song,

To such a deep delight 'twould win me,

That with music loud and long,

I would build that dome in air,

That sunny dome! those caves of ice!

And all who heard should see them there,

And all should cry, Beware! Beware!

His flashing eyes, his floating hair!

Weave a circle round him thrice,

And close your eyes with holy dread,

For he on honey-dew hath fed,

And drunk the milk of Paradise.

ROBERT SOUTHEY (1772-1843)

The third and least remembered of the Lake Poets, Southey was Poet Laureate for thirty years and much of his output reflects the demands put upon him by this office, which he came to detest. This poem is remarkable chiefly for being the inspiration for Lewis Carroll's more familiar parody.

THE OLD MAN'S COMFORTS
AND HOW HE GAINED THEM

You are old, Father William, the young man cried,

The few locks which are left you are grey;

You are hale, Father William, a hearty old man,

Now tell me the reason, I pray.

In the days of my youth, Father William replied,

I remember'd that youth would fly fast,

And abused not my health and my vigour at first,

That I never might need them at last.

You are old, Father William, the young man cried,

And pleasures with youth pass away;

And yet you lament not the days that are gone,

Now tell me the reason, I pray.

In the days of my youth, Father William replied,

I remember'd that youth could not last;

I thought of the future, whatever I did,

That I never might grieve for the past.

You are old, Father William, the young man cried,

And life must be hastening away;

You are cheerful, and love to converse upon death,

Now tell me the reason, I pray.

I am cheerful, young man, Father William replied,

Let the cause thy attention engage;

In the days of my youth I remember'd my God!

And He hath not forgotten my age.

FRANCIS SCOTT KEY (1779-1843)

While Romanticism was taking hold in Britain, the infant United States
were more concerned with patriotism and national identity. Francis Scott Key,
a lawyer in the District of Columbia, was inspired to pen his country's
future national anthem after watching the British attack on Baltimore in 1814.
The tune to which these words are sung was once a famous drinking song.

THE STAR-SPANGLED BANNER

O! say, can you see, by the dawn's early light,
What so proudly we hailed at the twilight's last gleaming –
Whose broad stripes and bright stars, through the clouds of the fight,
O'er the ramparts we watched were so gallantly streaming!
And the rocket's red glare, the bombs bursting in air,
Gave proof through the night that our flag was still there;
O! say, does that star-spangled banner yet wave
O'er the land of the free, and the home of the brave?

On that shore dimly seen through the mists of the deep,
Where the foe's haughty host in dread silence reposes,
What is that which the breeze, o'er the towering steep,
As it fitfully blows, now conceals, now discloses?
Now it catches the gleam of the morning's first beam,
In full glory reflected now shines on the stream;
'Tis the star-spangled banner; O long may it wave
O'er the land of the free, and the home of the brave!

And where is that band who so vauntingly swore
That the havoc of war and the battle's confusion
A home and a country should leave us no more?
Their blood has washed out their foul footsteps' pollution.
No refuge could save the hireling and slave
From the terror of flight, or the gloom of the grave;
And the star-spangled banner in triumph doth wave
O'er the land of the free, and the home of the brave.

O! thus be it ever, when freemen shall stand

Between their loved homes and the war's desolation!

Blest with victory and peace, may the heav'n-rescued land

Praise the power that hath made and preserved us a nation.

Then conquer we must, when our cause it is just,

And this be our motto – '*In God is our trust*':

And the star-spangled banner in triumph shall wave

O'er the land of the free, and the home of the brave.

Romanticism was not only a literary movement – it was born out of the political upheaval engendered by the American and French Revolutions, and it espoused causes based on the ideals of liberty and equality. Its subject matter ranged over the relationship between man and nature, happy and unhappy love, childhood and the creative process itself. Its heyday can be seen in the brief but glorious careers of Byron, Keats and Shelley.

GEORGE GORDON, LORD BYRON (1788-1824)

GROWING OLD

But now at thirty years my hair is grey –

(I wonder what it will be like at forty?

I thought of a peruke the other day –)

My heart is not much greener; and, in short, I

Have squandered my whole summer while 'twas May,

And feel no more the spirit to retort; I

Have spent my life, both interest and principal,
And deem not, what I deemed, my soul invincible.

No more – no more – Oh! never more on me
The freshness of the heart can fall like dew,
Which out of all the lovely things we see
Extracts emotions beautiful and new;
Hived in our bosoms like the bag o' the bee.
Think'st thou the honey with those objects grew?
Alas! 'twas not in them, but in thy power
To double even the sweetness of a flower.

No more – no more – Oh! never more, my heart,
Canst thou be my sole world, my universe!
Once all in all, but now a thing apart,
Thou canst not be my blessing or my curse:
The illusion's gone for ever, and thou art
Insensible, I trust, but none the worse,
And in thy stead I've got a deal of judgement,
Though Heaven knows how it ever found a lodgement.

My days of love are over; me no more
The charms of maid, wife, and still less of widow,
Can make the fool of which they made before, –
In short, I must not lead the life I did do;
The credulous hope of mutual minds is o'er,
The copious use of claret is forbid too,
So for a good old-gentlemanly vice,
I think I must take up with avarice.

Ambition was my idol, which was broken
Before the shrines of Sorrow, and of Pleasure;
And the two last have left me many a token
O'er which reflection may be made at leisure:
Now, like Friar Bacon's Brazen Head, I've spoken,
'Time is, Time was, Time's past': a chymic treasure
Is glittering Youth, which I have spent betimes –
My heart in passion, and my head on rhymes.

What is the end of Fame? 'tis but to fill
A certain portion of uncertain paper:
Some liken it to climbing up a hill,
Whose summit, like all hills, is lost in vapour;
For this men write, speak, preach, and heroes kill,
And bards burn what they call their 'midnight taper',
To have, when the original is dust,
A name, a wretched picture and worse bust.

What are the hopes of man? Old Egypt's King
Cheops erected the first Pyramid
And largest, thinking it was just the thing
To keep his memory whole, and mummy hid;
But somebody or other rummaging,
Burglariously broke his coffin's lid:
Let not a monument give you or me hopes,
Since not a pinch of dust remains of Cheops.

But I, being fond of true philosophy,
Say very often to myself, 'Alas!

OPPOSITE. SELF-PORTRAIT BY FRANZ VON LENBACH

All things that have been born were born to die,
And flesh (which Death mows down to hay) is grass;
You've passed your youth not so unpleasantly,
And if you had it o'er again – 'twould pass –
So thank your stars that matters are no worse,
And read your Bible, sir, and mind your purse.'

PERCY BYSSHE SHELLEY (1792-1822)

TO A SKYLARK

Hail to thee, blithe Spirit!
Bird thou never wert,
That from Heaven, or near it,
Pourest thy full heart
In profuse strains of unpremeditated art.

Higher still and higher
From the earth thou springest
Like a cloud of fire;
The blue deep thou wingest,
And singing still dost soar, and soaring ever singest.

In the golden lightning
Of the sunken sun,
O'er which clouds are bright'ning,
Thou dost float and run;
Like an unbodied joy whose race is just begun.

The pale purple even

Melts around thy flight;

Like a star of Heaven,

In the broad daylight

Thou art unseen, but yet I hear thy shrill delight,

Keen as are the arrows

Of that silver sphere,

Whose intense lamp narrows

In the white dawn clear

Until we hardly see – we feel that it is there.

All the earth and air

With thy voice is loud,

As, when night is bare,

From one lonely cloud

The moon rains out her beams, and Heaven is overflowed.

What thou art we know not;

What is most like thee?

From rainbow clouds there flow not

Drops so bright to see

As from thy presence showers a rain of melody.–

Like a poet hidden

In the light of thought

Singing hymns unbidden,

Till the world is wrought

To sympathy with hopes and fears it heeded not:

Like a high-born maiden

In a palace tower,

Soothing her love-laden

Soul in secret hour

With music sweet as love, which overflows her bower:

Like a glow-worm golden

In a dell of dew,

Scattering unbeholden

Its aerial hue

Among the flowers and grass which screen it from the view:

Like a rose embowered

In its own green leaves,

By warm winds deflowered,

Till the scent it gives

Makes faint with too much sweet these heavy-winged thieves:

Sound of vernal showers

On the twinkling grass,

Rain-awakened flowers –

All that ever was

Joyous and clear and fresh – thy music doth surpass.

Teach us, sprite or bird,

What sweet thoughts are thine:

I have never heard

Praise of love or wine

That panted forth a flood of rapture so divine.

Chorus hymeneal,

Or triumphal chant,

Matched with thine would be all

But an empty vaunt –

A thing wherein we feel there is some hidden want.

What objects are the fountains

Of thy happy strain?

What fields, or waves, or mountains?

What shapes of sky or plain?

What love of thine own kind? what ignorance of pain?

With thy clear keen joyance

Languor cannot be:

Shadow of annoyance

Never came near thee:

Thou lovest, but ne'er knew love's sad satiety.

Waking or asleep,

Thou of death must deem

Things more true and deep

Than we mortals dream,

Or how could thy notes flow in such a crystal stream?

We look before and after,

And pine for what is not:

Our sincerest laughter

With some pain is fraught;

Our sweetest songs are those that tell of saddest thought.

Yet, if we could scorn

Hate and pride and fear,

If we were things born

Not to shed a tear,

I know not how thy joy we ever should come near.

Better than all measures

Of delightful sound,

Better than all treasures

That in books are found,

Thy skill to poet were, thou scorner of the ground!

Teach me half the gladness

That thy brain must know;

Such harmonious madness

From my lips would flow,

The world should listen then, as I am listening now.

OZYMANDIAS

I met a traveller from an antique land

Who said: Two vast and trunkless legs of stone

Stand in the desert. Near them, on the sand,

Half sunk, a shattered visage lies, whose frown,

And wrinkled lip, and sneer of cold command,

Tell that its sculptor well those passions read

Which yet survive, stamped on these lifeless things,

The hand that mocked them, and the heart that fed:

THE ARCH OF TITUS IN ROME BY FRANZ VON LENBACH

And on the pedestal these words appear
'My name is Ozymandias, king of kings:
Look on my works, ye Mighty, and despair!'
Nothing beside remains. Round the decay
Of that colossal wreck, boundless and bare
The lone and level sands stretch far away.

ODE TO THE WEST WIND

O Wild West Wind, thou breath of Autumn's being,
Thou from whose unseen presence the leaves dead
Are driven like ghosts from an enchanter fleeing,

Yellow, and black, and pale, and hectic red,
Pestilence-stricken multitudes! O thou
Who chariotest to their dark wintry bed

The wingèd seeds, where they lie cold and low,
Each like a corpse within its grave, until
Thine azure sister of the Spring shall blow

Her clarion o'er the dreaming earth, and fill
(Driving sweet buds like flocks to feed in air)
With living hues and odours plain and hill;

Wild Spirit, which art moving everywhere;
Destroyer and preserver; hear, O hear!

Thou on whose stream, 'mid the steep sky's commotion,

Loose clouds like earth's decaying leaves are shed,

Shook from the tangled boughs of heaven and ocean,

Angels of rain and lightning! there are spread

On the blue surface of thine airy surge,

Like the bright hair uplifted from the head

Of some fierce Maenad, even from the dim verge

Of the horizon to the zenith's height,

The locks of the approaching storm. Thou dirge

Of the dying year, to which this closing night

Will be the dome of a vast sepulchre,

Vaulted with all thy congregated might

Of vapours, from whose solid atmosphere

Black rain and fire, and hail will burst: O hear!

Thou who didst waken from his summer dreams

The blue Mediterranean, where he lay,

Lulled by the coil of his crystalline streams,

Beside a pumice isle in Baiae's bay,

And saw in sleep old palaces and towers

Quivering within the wave's intenser day,

All overgrown with azure moss, and flowers

So sweet, the sense faints picturing them! Thou

For whose path the Atlantic's level powers

Cleave themselves into chasms, while far below
The sea-blooms and the oozy woods which wear
The sapless foliage of the ocean, know

Thy voice, and suddenly grow gray with fear,
And tremble and despoil themselves: O hear!

If I were a dead leaf thou mightest bear;
If I were a swift cloud to fly with thee;
A wave to pant beneath thy power, and share

The impulse of thy strength, only less free
Than thou, O uncontrollable! if even
I were as in my boyhood, and could be

The comrade of thy wanderings over heaven,
As then, when to outstrip thy skiey speed
Scarce seemed a vision – I would ne'er have striven

As thus with thee in prayer in my sore need.
O! lift me as a wave, a leaf, a cloud!
I fall upon the thorns of life! I bleed!

A heavy weight of hours has chained and bowed
One too like thee – tameless, and swift, and proud.

Make me thy lyre, even as the forest is:
What if my leaves are falling like its own?
The tumult of thy mighty harmonies

Will take from both a deep autumnal tone,
Sweet though in sadness. Be thou, Spirit fierce,
My spirit! Be thou me, impetuous one!

Drive my dead thoughts over the universe,
Like withered leaves, to quicken a new birth
And, by the incantation of this verse,

Scatter, as from an unextinguished hearth
Ashes and sparks, my words among mankind!
Be through my lips to unawakened ear

The trumpet of a prophecy! O Wind,
If Winter comes, can Spring be far behind?

JOHN KEATS (1795-1821)

ON FIRST LOOKING INTO CHAPMAN'S HOMER

Much have I travelled in the realms of gold,
And many goodly states and kingdoms seen;
Round many western islands have I been
Which bards in fealty to Apollo hold.
Oft of one wide expanse had I been told
That deep-browed Homer ruled as his demesne;
Yet did I never breathe its pure serene
Till I heard Chapman speak out loud and bold:
Then felt I like some watcher of the skies

When a new planet swims into his ken;
Or like stout Cortez when with eagle eyes
He stared at the Pacific – and all his men
Looked at each other with a wild surmise
Silent, upon a peak in Darien

ENDYMION (extract)

A thing of beauty is a joy for ever:
Its loveliness increases, it will never
Pass into nothingness; but still will keep
A bower quiet for us, and a sleep
Full of sweet dreams, and health, and quiet breathing.
Therefore, on every morrow, are we wreathing
A flowery band to bind us to the earth,
Spite of despondence, of the inhuman dearth
Of noble natures, of the gloomy days,
Of all the unhealthy and o'er-darkened ways
Made of our searching; yes, in spite of all
Some shape of beauty moves away the pall
From our dark spirits.

TO AUTUMN

Season of mists and mellow fruitfulness,
Close bosom-friend of the maturing sun;
Conspiring with him how to load and bless
With fruit the vines that round the thatch-eaves run;

To bend with apples the mossed cottage-trees,
And fill all fruit with ripeness to the core;
To swell the gourd, and plump the hazel shells
With a sweet kernel; to set budding more,
And still more, later flowers for the bees,
Until they think warm days will never cease,
For Summer has o'er-brimmed their clammy cells.

Who hath not seen thee oft amid thy store?
Sometimes whoever seeks abroad may find
Thee sitting careless on a granary floor,
Thy hair soft-lifted by the winnowing wind;
Or on a half-reaped furrow sound asleep,
Drowsed with the fume of poppies, while thy hook
Spares the next swath and all its twinèd flowers:
And sometimes like a gleaner thou dost keep
Steady thy laden head across a brook;
Or by a cider-press, with patient look,
Thou watchest the last oozings hours by hours.

Where are the songs of Spring? Aye, where are they?
Think not of them, thou hast thy music too –
While barrèd clouds bloom the soft-dying day,
And touch the stubble-plains with rosy hue;
Then in a wailful choir the small gnats mourn
Among the river sallows, borne aloft
Or sinking as the light wind lives or dies;
And full-grown lambs loud bleat from hilly bourn;
Hedge crickets sing; and now with treble soft
The redbreast whistles from a garden-croft;
And gathering swallows twitter in the skies.

*Thomas Hood and John Clare have been overshadowed by their great
contemporaries, but both were prolific writers who enjoyed considerable
success in their day. Hood's works ranged from serious social comment
to humorous verse, while Clare is best remembered for poems evoking
a rural England threatened by the onset of the Industrial Revolution.*

THOMAS HOOD (1799-1845)

I REMEMBER, I REMEMBER

I remember, I remember,
The house where I was born,
The little window where the sun
Came peeping in at morn;
He never came a wink too soon,
Nor brought too long a day,
But now, I often wish the night
Had borne my breath away!
I remember, I remember,
The roses, red and white,
The violets, and the lily-cups,
Those flowers made of light!
The lilacs where the robin built,
And where my brother set
The laburnum on his birthday, –
The tree is living yet!

OPPOSITE. THE HAY RICK BY MYLES BIRKET FOSTER

I remember, I remember,
Where I was used to swing,
And thought the air must rush as fresh
To swallows on the wing;
My spirit flew in feathers then,
That is so heavy now,
And summer pools could hardly cool
The fever on my brow!

JOHN CLARE (1793-1864)

I am: yet what I am none cares or knows,
My friends forsake me like a memory lost;
I am the self-consumer of my woes,
They rise and vanish in oblivious host,
Like shades in love and death's oblivion lost;
And yet I am, and live with shadows tost

Into the nothingness of scorn and noise,
Into the living sea of waking dreams,
Where there is neither sense of life nor joys,
But the vast shipwreck of my life's esteems;
And e'en the dearest – that I loved the best –
Are strange – nay, rather stranger than the rest.

I long for scenes where man has never trod,
A place where woman never smiled or wept;
There to abide with my Creator, God,

And sleep as I in childhood sweetly slept:
Untroubling and untroubled where I lie,
The grass below – above the vaulted sky.

᪥

*The mid-nineteenth century saw a great flowering of American poets and philosophers,
anxious to shake off the influence of Europe which they felt had shackled them
too long. As Emerson put it, 'We will walk on our own feet, we will work with our own
hands, we will speak with our own minds.' He and his younger friend Thoreau
abandoned their Christian upbringings in favour of a creed they called
Transcendentalism, a combination of mysticism and natural philosophy,
in which nature and the individual were seen as being inseparable from God.
Thoreau experimented with self-sufficiency at Walden, near his home town of
Concord, Massachusetts, and wrote an influential book on the subject.*

*Longfellow belongs much more to the mainstream, having spent many years
teaching at Harvard, but he is one of the most popular of American poets and
'The Song of Hiawatha' one of the best known of American poems.*

*Whitman ranks among the greatest of American poets, following closely on
Emerson's heels in his desire to establish an American voice unfettered by
European or Asian antecedents. His collection* Leaves of Grass *was
hailed by Emerson as 'the most extraordinary piece of wit and wisdom that
America has yet contributed'. His sharp tongue earned him many enemies: it was he
who, in response to Oscar Wilde's wistful remark, 'I wish I had said that',
famously retorted, 'You will, Oscar, you will.'*

RALPH WALDO EMERSON (1803-1882)

EARTH-SONG

'Mine and yours;

Mine, not yours.

Earth endures;

Stars abide

Shine down in the old sea;

Old are the shores;

But where are old men?

I who have seen much,

Such have I never seen.

'The lawyer's deed

Ran sure,

In tail,

To them, and to their heirs

Who shall succeed,

Without fail,

Forevermore.

'Here is the land,

Shaggy with wood,

With its old valley,

Mound and flood.

But the heritors?

Fled like the flood's foam.

The lawyer, and the laws,

OPPOSITE. LANDSCAPE BY ROBERT FOWLER

And the kingdom,
Clean swept herefrom.

'They called me theirs,
Who so controlled me;
Yet every one
Wished to stay, and is gone,
How am I theirs,
If they cannot hold me,
But I hold them?'

When I heard the Earth-song
I was no longer brave;
My avarice cooled
Like lust in the chill of the grave.

BRAHMA

If the red slayer think he slays,
Or if the slain think he is slain,
They know not well the subtle ways
I keep, and pass, and turn again.

Far or forgot to me is near,
Shadow and sunlight are the same;
The vanquished gods to me appear,
And one to me are shame and fame.

They reckon ill who leave me out;
When me they fly, I am the wings;
I am the doubter and the doubt
And I the hymn the Brahmin sings.

The strong gods pine for my abode,
And pine in vain the sacred Seven,
But thou, meek lover of the good!
Find me, and turn thy back on heaven.

HENRY WADSWORTH LONGFELLOW (1807-1882)

THE SONG OF HIAWATHA (extract)

Heavy with the heat and silence
Grew the afternoon of Summer;
With a drowsy sound the forest

Whispered round the sultry wigwam,
With a sound of sleep the water
Rippled on the beach below it;
From the cornfields shrill and ceaseless
Sang the grasshopper, Pahpuk-keena;
And the guests of Hiawatha,
Weary with the heat of Summer,
Slumbered in the sultry wigwam.

Slowly o'er the simmering landscape
Fell the evening's dusk and coolness,
And the long and level sunbeams
Shot their spears into the forest,
Breaking through its shields of shadow,
Rushed into each secret ambush,
Searched each thicket, dingle, hollow;
Still the guests of Hiawatha
Slumbered in the silent wigwam.

From his place rose Hiawatha,
Bade farewell to old Nokomis,
Spake in whispers, spake in this wise,
Did not wake the guests, that slumbered:
'I am going, O Nokomis,
On a long and distant journey,
To the portals of the Sunset,
To the regions of the home-wind,
Of the Northwest-Wind, Keewaydin.
But these guests I leave behind me,
In your watch and ward I leave them;
See that never harm comes near them

See that never fear molests them,
Never danger nor suspicion,
Never want of food or shelter,
In the lodge of Hiawatha!'

Forth into the village went he,
Bade farewell to all the warriors,
Bade farewell to all the young men,
Spake persuading, spake in this wise:
'I am going, O my people,
On a long and distant journey;
Many moons and many winters
Will have come, and will have vanished,
Ere I come again to see you.
But my guests I leave behind me;
Listen to their words of wisdom,
Listen to the truth they tell you,
For the Master of Life has sent them
From the land of light and morning!'

On the shore stood Hiawatha,
Turned and waved his hand at parting;
On the clear and luminous water
Launched his birch canoe for sailing,
From the pebbles of the margin
Shoved it forth into the water;
Whispered to it, 'Westward! westward!'
And with speed it darted forward.
And the evening sun descending
Set the clouds on fire with redness,

Burned the broad sky, like a prairie,
Left upon the level water
One long track and trail of splendor,
Down whose stream, as down a river,
Westward, westward Hiawatha
Sailed into the fiery sunset,
Sailed into the purple vapors,
Sailed into the dusk of evening.
And the people from the margin
Watched him floating, rising, sinking,
Till the birch canoe seemed lifted
High into that sea of splendor,
Till it sank into the vapors
Like the new moon slowly, slowly
Sinking in the purple distance.

And they said, 'Farewell forever!'
Said, 'Farewell, O Hiawatha!'
And the forests, dark and lonely,
Moved through all their depths of darkness,
Sighed, 'Farewell, O Hiawatha!'
And the waves upon the margin
Rising, rippling on the pebbles,
Sobbed, 'Farewell, O Hiawatha!'
And the heron, the Shuhshuhgah,
From her haunts among the fen-lands,
Screamed, 'Farewell, O Hiawatha!'

Thus departed Hiawatha,
Hiawatha the Beloved,

In the glory of the sunset,

In the purple mists of evening,

To the regions of the home-wind,

Of the Northwest-Wind, Keewaydin,

To the Islands of the Blessed,

To the kingdom of Ponemah,

To the land of the Hereafter!

HENRY DAVID THOREAU (1817-1862)

I AM A PARCEL OF VAIN STRIVINGS TIED

I am a parcel of vain strivings tied

By a chance bond together,

Dangling this way and that, their links

Were made so loose and wide,

Methinks,

For milder weather.

A bunch of violets without their roots,

And sorrel intermixed,

Encircled by a wisp of straw

Once coiled about their shoots,

The law

By which I'm fixed.

A nosegay which Time clutched from out

Those fair Elysian fields,

With weeds and broken stems, in haste,

Doth make the rabble rout

That waste

The day he yields.

And here I bloom for a short hour unseen,

Drinking my juices up,

With no root in the land

To keep my branches green,

But stand

In a bare cup.

Some tender buds were left upon my stem

In mimicry of life,

But ah! the children will not know,

Till time has withered them,

The woe

With which they're rife.

But now I see I was not plucked for naught,

And after in life's vase

Of glass set while I might survive,

But by a kind hand brought

Alive

To a strange place.

That stock thus thinned will soon redeem its hours,

And by another year,

Such as God knows, with freer air,

More fruits and fairer flowers

Will bear,

While I droop here.

WALT WHITMAN (1819-1892)

SONG OF MYSELF (extract)

I celebrate myself, and sing myself,
And what I assume you shall assume,
For every atom belonging to me as good belongs to you.

I loafe and invite my soul
I lean and loafe at my ease observing a spear of summer grass.

My tongue, every atom of my blood, form'd from this soil, this air,
Born here of parents born here from parents the same,
and their parents the same,
I, now thirty-seven years old in perfect health begin,
Hoping to cease not till death.

Creeds and schools in abeyance,
Retiring back a while suffced at what they are, but never forgotten,
I harbor for good or bad, I permit to speak at every hazard,
Nature without check with original energy.

᠁

OPPOSITE. WOODLAND SCENE BY WIILLIAM FULTON BROWN

MEMORIES OF PRESIDENT LINCOLN (extracts)

O Captain! my Captain! our fearful trip is done,
The ship has weathered every rack, the prize we sought is won,
The port is near, the bells I hear, the people all exulting,
While follow eyes the steady keel, the vessel grim and daring,
But O heart! heart! heart!
O the bleeding drops of red!
Where on the deck my Captain lies,
Fallen cold and dead

O Captain! my Captain! rise up and hear the bells;
Rise up – for you the flag is flung – for you the bugle trills,
For you bouquets and ribboned wreaths – for you the shores a-crowding,
For you they call, the swaying mass, their eager faces turning,
Here, Captain! dear father!
This arm beneath your head!
It is some dream that on the deck
You've fallen cold and dead.

My Captain does not answer, his lips are pale and still,
My father does not feel my arm, he has no pulse nor will;
The ship is anchored safe and sound, its voyage closed and done,
From fearful trip the victor ship comes in with object won;
Exult, O shores! and ring, O bells!
But I, with mournful tread,
Walk the deck my Captain lies,
Fallen cold and dead.

OPPOSITE. WINTRY CHURCHYARD

When Lilacs Last in the Dooryard Bloom'd

Come, lovely and soothing Death,
Undulate round the world, serenely arriving, arriving,
In the day, in the night, to all, to each,
Sooner or later, delicate Death.

Praised be the fathomless universe
For life and joy, and for objects and knowledge curious;
And for love, sweet love – But praise! O praise and praise
For the sure-enwinding arms of cool-enfolding Death.

Dark Mother, always gliding near, with soft feet,
Have none chanted for thee a chant of fullest welcome?
Then I chant it for thee – I glorify thee above all;
I bring thee a song, that, when thou must indeed come, thou come unfalteringly.
Approach, encompassing Death – strong deliveress!
When it is so – when thou hast taken them, I joyously sing the dead
Lost in the loving, floating ocean of thee,
Laved in the flood of thy bliss, O Death.

ALFRED, LORD TENNYSON (1809-1892)

The work and influence of Tennyson dominates English poetry in the latter part of the nineteenth century. Poet Laureate from 1850 until his death, he produced a vast amount of verse of vastly varying quality. 'In Memoriam', written after the tragically early death of his close friend Arthur Hallam, is probably his most touching work. His reputation is also maintained by 'Idylls of the King', a massive work based on the legends of King Arthur. 'The Lady of Shalott', although not part of the 'Idylls', draws on the same background.

IN MEMORIAM (EXTRACT)

I envy not in any moods
The captive void of noble rage,
The linnet born within the cage,
That never knew the summer woods:

I envy not the beast that takes
His license in the field of time,
Unfetter'd by the sense of crime,
To whom a conscience never wakes;
Nor, what may count itself as blest,
The heart that never plighted troth
But stagnates in the weeds of sloth,
Nor any want-begotten rest.

I hold it true, whate'er befall;
I feel it when I sorrow most;
'Tis better to have loved and lost
Than never to have loved at all.

THE LADY OF SHALOTT (extract)

Part I

On either side the river lie
Long fields of barley and of rye,
That clothe the wold and meet the sky;
And through the field the road runs by
To many-towered Camelot;
And up and down the people go,
Gazing where the lilies blow
Round an island there below,
The island of Shalott.

Willows whiten, aspens quiver,
Little breezes dusk and shiver
Through the wave that runs for ever
By the island in the river
Flowing down to Camelot.
Four gray walls, and four gray towers,
Overlook a space of flowers,
And the silent isle imbowers
The Lady of Shalott.

By the margin, willow-veiled,
Slide the heavy barges trailed
By slow horses; and unhailed
The shallop flitteth silken-sailed
Skimming down to Camelot:
But who hath seen her wave her hand?

Or at the casement seen her stand?

Or is she known in all the land,

The Lady of Shalott?…

Part II

There she weaves by night and day

A magic web with colours gay.

She has heard a whisper say,

A curse is on her if she stay

To look down to Camelot.

She knows not what the curse may be,

And so she weaveth steadily,

And little other care hath she,

The Lady of Shalott.

And moving through a mirror clear

That hangs before her all the year,

Shadows of the world appear.

There she sees the highway near

Winding down to Camelot:

There the river eddy whirls,

And there the surly village-churls,

And the red cloaks of market girls,

Pass onward from Shalott.

Sometimes a troop of damsels glad,

An abbot on an ambling pad,

Sometimes a curly shepherd-lad,

OPPOSITE. THE LADY OF SHALOTT BY WILLIAM HOLMAN HUNT

Or long-haired page in crimson clad,
Goes by to towered Camelot;
And sometimes through the mirror blue
The knights come riding two and two:
She hath no loyal knight and true,
The Lady of Shalott.

But in her web she still delights
To weave the mirror's magic sights,
For often through the silent nights
A funeral, with plumes and lights
And music, went to Camelot:
Or when the moon was overhead,
Came two young lovers lately wed;
'I am half sick of shadows,' said
The Lady of Shalott.

Part III
A bow-shot from her bower-eaves,
He rode between the barley-sheaves,
The sun came dazzling through the leaves
And flamed upon the brazen greaves
Of bold Sir Lancelot.
A red-cross knight for ever kneeled
To a lady in his shield,
That sparkled on the yellow field,
Beside remote Shalott...

All in the blue unclouded weather
Thick-jewelled shone the saddle-leather,

The helmet and the helmet-feather
Burned like one burning flame together,
As he rode down to Camelot.
As often through the purple night,
Below the starry clusters bright,
Some bearded meteor, trailing light,
Moves over still Shalott.

His broad clear brow in sunlight glowed;
On burnished hooves his war-horse trode;
From underneath his helmet flowed
His coal-black curls as on he rode,
As he rode down to Camelot.
From the bank and from the river
He flashed into the crystal mirror,
'Tirra lirra,' by the river
Sang Sir Lancelot.

She left the web, she left the loom,
She made three paces through the room,
She saw the water-lily bloom,
She saw the helmet and the plume,
She looked down to Camelot.
Out flew the web and floated wide;
The mirror cracked from side to side;
'The curse is come upon me,' cried
The Lady of Shalott.

Part IV

In the stormy east-wind straining,
The pale yellow woods were waning,
The broad stream in his banks complaining,
Heavily the low sky raining
Over towered Camelot;
Down she came and found a boat
Beneath a willow left afloat,
And round about the prow she wrote
The Lady of Shalott.

And down the river's dim expanse
Like some bold seer in a trance,
Seeing all his own mischance –
With a glassy countenance
Did she look to Camelot.
And at the closing of the day
She loosed the chain, and down she lay;
The broad stream bore her far away,
The Lady of Shalott.

Lying, robed in snowy white
That loosely flew to left and right –
The leaves upon her falling light –
Through the noises of the night
She floated down to Camelot:
And as the boat-head wound along
The willowy hills and fields among,
They heard her singing her last song,
The Lady of Shalott.

Heard a carol, mournful, holy,
Chanted loudly, chanted lowly,
Till her blood was frozen slowly,
And her eyes were darkened wholly,
Turned to towered Camelot.
For ere she reached upon the tide
The first house by the water-side,
Singing in her song she died,
The Lady of Shalott.

Under tower and balcony,
By garden-wall and gallery,
A gleaming shape she floated by,
Dead-pale between the houses high,
Silent into Camelot.
Out upon the wharfs they came,
Knight and burgher, lord and dame,
And round the prow they read her name,
The Lady of Shalott.

Who is this? and what is here?
And in the lighted palace near
Died the sound of royal cheer;
And they crossed themselves for fear,
All the knights at Camelot:
But Lancelot mused a little space;
He said, 'She has a lovely face;
God in his mercy lend her grace,
The Lady of Shalott.'

❧

The Brownings, husband and wife, were the chief characters in a famous romance which
featured a despotic father, a clandestine marriage and an escape from London to Italy,
where they lived for most of the rest of her life and entertained many visitors from the
English artistic world. She in particular was hailed a great poet in her lifetime;
his works have gone in and out of fashion, but the one included here
has a wistful homesickness that makes it a perennial favourite.

ELIZABETH BARRETT BROWNING (1806-1861)

GRIEF

I tell you, hopeless grief is passionless;
That only men incredulous of despair,
Half-taught in anguish, through the midnight air
Beat upward to God's throne in loud access
Of shrieking and reproach. Full desertness
In souls as countries lieth silent-bare
Under the blanching, vertical eye-glare
Of the absolute Heavens. Deep-hearted man, express
Grief for thy Dead in silence like to Death –
Most like a monumental statue set
In everlasting watch and moveless woe
Till itself crumble to the dust beneath.
Touch it; the marble eyelids are not wet:
If it could weep, it could arise and go.

❧❧❧

ROBERT BROWNING (1812-1889)

HOME-THOUGHTS, FROM ABROAD

O to be in England
Now that April's there,
And whoever wakes in England
Sees, some morning, unaware,
That the lowest boughs and the brushwood sheaf
Round the elm-tree bole are in tiny leaf,
While the chaffinch sings on the orchard bough
In England – now!

And after April, when May follows,
And the whitethroat builds, and all the swallows!
Hark, where my blossomed pear-tree in the hedge
Leans to the field and scatters on the clover
Blossoms and dewdrops – at the bent spray's edge –
That's the wise thrush; he sings each song twice over,
Lest you should think he never could recapture
The first fine careless rapture!
And though the fields look rough with hoary dew,
All will be gay when noontide wakes anew
The buttercups, the little children's dower
– Far brighter than this gaudy melon-flower!

❧❀❧

EMILY BRONTË (1818-1848)

Emly Brontë was the finest poet of her famous family. Like her sisters
Charlotte and Anne, she was strongly influenced by the wild Yorkshire moors
on which they were brought up, and by the threat of death which seems
to have hovered permanently over them. Happiest living a quiet life
in her father's parsonage, she was obviously a woman of great
moral courage and faced the prospect of her own premature
death without complaint.

THE PHILOSOPHER

Enough of thought, philosopher!
Too long hast thou been dreaming
Unlightened in this chamber drear
While summer's sun is beaming!
Space-sweeping soul, what sad refrain
Concludes thy musings once again?
'Oh, for the time when I shall sleep
Without identity,
And never care how rain may steep,
Or snow may cover me!
No promised heaven, these wild desires
Could all, or half fulfil;
No threatened hell, with quenchless fires,
Subdue this quenchless will!'
'So said I, and still say the same;
Still, to my death, will say
Three gods, within this little frame,

Are warring, night and day;
Heaven could not hold them all, and yet
They all are held in me;
And must be mine till I forget
My present entity!
Oh, for the time, when in my breast
Their struggles will be o'er!
Oh, for the day, when I shall rest,
And never suffer more!'

'I saw a spirit, standing, man,
Where thou dost stand – an hour ago,
And round his feet three rivers ran,
Of equal depth, and equal flow
A golden stream – and one like blood;
And one like sapphire seemed to be;
But where they joined their triple flood
It tumbled in an inky sea.
The spirit sent his dazzling gaze
Down through that ocean's gloomy night;
Then, kindling all, with sudden blaze,
The glad deep sparkled wide and bright
White as the sun, far, far more fair
Than its divided sources were!'

'And even for that spirit, seer,
I've watched and sought my lifetime long;
Sought him in heaven, hell, earth, and air,
An endless search, and always wrong.
Had I but seen his glorious eye

Once light the clouds that 'wilder me,

I ne'er had raised this coward cry

To cease to think, and cease to be;

I ne'er had called oblivion blest,

Nor, stretching eager hands to death,

Implored to change for senseless rest

This sentient soul, this living breath.

Oh, let me die – that power and will

Their cruel strife may close;

And conquered good and conquering ill

Be lost in one repose!'

MATTHEW ARNOLD (1822-1888)

The son of a famous father – the headmaster of Rugby featured in Tom Brown's
Schooldays *– Matthew Arnold's poetry was mostly written before he was forty. His
principal reputation nowadays is as a critic. He believed that England was suffering from
literary and social small-mindedness and needed more intellectual curiosity.*

DOVER BEACH

The sea is calm tonight.

The tide is full, the moon lies fair

Upon the straits; on the French coast the light

Gleams and is gone; the cliffs of England stand,

Glimmering and vast, out in the tranquil bay.

Come to the window, sweet is the night-air!

Only, from the long line of spray

Where the sea meets the moon-blanched land,

Listen! you hear the grating roar

Of pebbles which the waves draw back, and fling,

At their return, up the high strand,

Begin, and cease, and then again begin

With tremulous cadence slow, and bring

The eternal note of sadness in.

Sophocles long ago

Heard it on the Aegean, and it brought

SEASCAPE IN KENT BY WIILIAM DYCE

Into his mind the turbid ebb and flow
Of human misery; we
Find also in the sound a thought,
Hearing it by this distant northern sea.

The Sea of Faith
Was once, too, at the full, and round earth's shore
Lay like the folds of a bright girdle furled.
But now I only hear
Its melancholy, long, withdrawing roar,
Retreating, to the breath
Of the night-wind, down the vast edges drear
And naked shingles of the world.

Ah, love, let us be true
To one another! for the world, which seems
To lie before us like a land of dreams,
So various, so beautiful, so new,
Hath really neither joy, nor love, nor light,
Nor certitude, nor peace, nor help for pain;
And we are here as on a darkling plain
Swept with confused alarms of struggle and flight,
Where ignorant armies clash by night.

EMILY DICKINSON (1830-1886)

*Mystery surrounds some of Emily Dickinson's writing, which she refused
to have published during her lifetime. Much of it is spiritual in content,
though some critics believe that some of it refers to an unhappy earthly passion.*

Whatever the interpretation, she remains – deservedly – one of America's most respected and most widely read poets.

'I DIED FOR BEAUTY – BUT WAS SCARCE'

I died for Beauty – but was scarce
Adjusted in the Tomb
When One who died for Truth, was lain
In an adjoining Room –
He questioned softly 'Why I failed'?
'For Beauty', I replied
'And I – for Truth – Themself are One
We Bretheren, are', He said –
And so, as Kinsmen, met a Night –
We talked between the Rooms
Until the Moss had reached out lips
And covered up – our names.

'MY LIFE CLOSED TWICE BEFORE ITS CLOSE'

My life closed twice before its close
It yet remains to see
If Immortality unveil
A third event to me
So huge, so hopeless to conceive
As these that twice befell.
Parting is all we know of heaven,
And all we need of hell.

GERARD MANLEY HOPKINS (1844-1889)

Gerard Manley Hopkins was a prolific poet in his youth, but on converting to Catholicism in his early twenties and subsequently becoming a Jesuit he symbolically burned most of his poems, though he sent some copies to a friend from his days as a student in Oxford, the poet Robert Bridges. Most of his best known poems date from the last years of his life and were published posthumously by Bridges.
Hopkins combined a deep love of God with an almost equal passion for the natural world, which he regarded as a manifestation of the Divine.

SPRING

Nothing is so beautiful as spring –
When weeds, in wheels, shoot long and lovely and lush;
Thrush's eggs look little low heavens, and thrush
Through the echoing timber does so rinse and wring
The ear, it strikes like lightnings to hear him sing,
The glassy peartree leaves and blooms, they brush
The descending blue; that blue is all in a rush
With richness; the racing lambs too have fair their fling.

What is all this juice and all this joy?
A strain of the earth's sweet being in the beginning
In Eden garden. – Have, get, before it cloy,
Before it cloud, Christ, lord, and sour with sinning,

Innocent mind and Mayday in girl and boy,
Most, O maid's child, thy choice and worthy the winning.

GOD'S GRANDEUR

The world is charged with the grandeur of God.
It will flame out, like shining from shook foil;
It gathers to a greatness, like the ooze of oil
Crushed. Why do men then now not reck his rod?
Generations have trod, have trod, have trod;
And all is seared with trade; bleared, smeared with toil;
And wears man's smudge and shares man's smell: the soil

Is bare now, nor can foot feel, being shod.
And for all this, nature is never spent;
There lives the dearest freshness deep down things;
And though the last lights off the black West went
Oh, morning, at the brown brink eastward, springs –
Because the Holy Ghost over the bent
World broods with warm breast and with ah! bright wings.

❦

PIED BEAUTY

Glory be to God for dappled things –
For skies of couple-colour as a brinded cow;

PIED SKY BY ROBERT FOWLER

For rose-moles all in stipple upon trout that swim;
Fresh fire-coal chestnut-falls; finches' wings;

Landscape plotted and pieced – fold, fallow, and plough;
And all trades, their gear and tackle and trim.

All things counter, original, spare, strange;
Whatever is fickle, freckled (who knows how?)
With swift, slow; sweet, sour; adazzle, dim;
He fathers-forth whose beauty is past change:
Praise him.

❦

Robert Louis Stevenson (1850-1894)

Born and brought up in Edinburgh, where the climate did nothing to help his sickly constitution, the author of Treasure Island *spent much of the latter part of his life abroad. He died on the Pacific island of Samoa where he had earned the nickname of 'Tusitala' – the storyteller.*

Requiem

Under the wide and starry sky
Dig the grave and let me lie:
Glad did I live and gladly die,
And I laid me down with a will.

This be the verse you grave for me:
Here he lies where he long'd to be;
Home is the sailor, home from sea,
And the hunter home from the hill.

Oscar Wilde (1854-1900)

Oscar Wilde's story is too well known to need repeating here. He wrote The Ballad of Reading Gaol *in 1898, when in exile in Paris after his release from prison. It is a bitter reflection on the love affair which led him to end his life in squalor, poverty and despair.*

THE BALLAD OF READING GAOL (extract)

Yet each man kills the thing he loves,

By each let this be heard,

Some do it with a bitter look,

Some with a flattering word,

The coward does it with a kiss,

The brave man with a sword!

Some kill their love when they are young,

And some when they are old;

Some strangle with the hands of Lust,

Some with the hands of Gold:

The kindest use a knife, because

The dead so soon grow cold.

Some love too little, some too long,

Some sell, and others buy;

Some do the deed with many tears,

And some without a sigh:

For each man kills the thing he loves,

Yet each man does not die.

He does not die a death of shame

On a day of dark disgrace,

Nor have a noose about his neck,

Nor a cloth upon his face,

Nor drop feet foremost through the floor

Into an empty space.

ૐ

RUDYARD KIPLING (1865-1936)

The Imperialist spirit of the era in which Kipling lived makes some of his poetry embarrassing to modern readers and overshadows his real qualities. He was extremely popular in his day and was awarded the Nobel Prize for Literature in 1907. His prose writing for children, notably The Jungle Book *and* Just So Stories, *is still widely read, and in 1995 the British public voted this their favourite poem.*

IF –

If you can keep your head when all about you
Are losing theirs and blaming it on you,
If you can trust yourself when all men doubt you,
But make allowance for their doubting too;
If you can wait and not be tired of waiting,
Or being lied about, don't deal in lies,
Or being hated, don't give way to hating,
And yet don't look too good, nor talk too wise:
If you can dream and not make dreams your master;
If you can think – and not make thoughts your aim;
If you can meet with Triumph and Disaster
And treat those two impostors just the same;
If you can bear to hear the truth you've spoken
Twisted by knaves to make a trap for fools,
Or watch the things you gave your life to, broken,
And stoop and build 'em up with worn-out tools:

If you can make one heap of all your winnings
And risk it on one turn of pitch-and-toss,

And lose, and start again at your beginnings
And never breathe a word about your loss;
If you can force your heart and nerve and sinew
To serve your turn long after they are gone,
And so hold on when there is nothing in you
Except the Will which says to them: 'Hold on!'

If you can talk with crowds and keep your virtue,
Or walk with Kings – nor lose the common touch,

If neither foes nor loving friends can hurt you,
If all men count with you, but none too much;
If you can fill the unforgiving minute
With sixty seconds' worth of distance run,
Yours is the Earth and everything that's in it,
And – which is more – you'll be a Man, my son!

WILLIAM BUTLER YEATS (1865-1939)

Possibly the greatest of Irish poets and an overwhelming influence on future generations, Yeats was a towering figure in literary and political circles, being one of the founders of the Abbey Theatre in Dublin, one of the first senators of the Irish Free State and a Nobel Laureate. Although he married Georgie Hyde-Lees in 1917, he is said to have nurtured a lifelong passion for Maude Gonne, a fellow Republican, who inspired much of his work.

OPPOSITE. FISHMERMAN'S HOME NEAR BALLYNAKILL BAY

THE LAKE ISLE OF INNISFREE

I will arise and go now, and go to Innisfree,
And a small cabin build there, of clay and wattles made;
Nine bean rows will I have there, a hive for the honey bee
And live alone in the bee-loud glade.

And I shall have some peace there, for peace comes dropping slow,
Dropping from the veils of the morning to where the cricket sings;
There midnight's all a glimmer, and noon a purple glow,
And evening full of the linnet's wings.

I will arise and go now, for always night and day
I hear lake water lapping with low sounds by the shore;
While I stand on the roadway, or on the pavements gray,
I hear it in the deep heart's core.

AMY LOWELL (1874-1925)

*Born in Massachusetts, Amy Lowell became one of the foremost exponents of a style
known as Imagism. This poem was inspired by love of her native New England.*

LILACS

Lilacs

False blue,

White,

Purple,

Colour of lilac,

Your great puffs of flowers

Are everywhere in this my New England.

Among your heart-shaped leaves

Orange orioles hop like music-box birds and sing

Their little weak soft songs;

In the crooks of your branches

The bright eyes of song sparrows sitting on spotted eggs

Peer restlessly through the light and shadow

Of all Springs.

Lilacs in dooryards

Holding quiet conversations with an early moon;

Lilacs watching a deserted house

Settling sideways into the grass of an old road;

Lilacs, wind-beaten, staggering under a lopsided shock of bloom

Above a cellar dug into a hill.

You are everywhere.

You were everywhere.

You tapped the window when the preacher preached his sermon,

And ran along the road beside the boy going to school.

You stood by pasture-bars to give the cows good milking,

You persuaded the housewife that her dish pan was of silver

And her husband an image of pure gold.

You flaunted the fragrance of your blossoms

Through the wide doors of Custom Houses—

You, and sandal-wood, and tea,

Charging the noses of quill-driving clerks

When a ship was in from China.

You called to them: 'Goose-quill men, goose-quill men,

May is a month for flitting,'

Until they writhed on their high stools

And wrote poetry on their letter-sheets behind the propped up ledgers.

Paradoxical New England clerks,

Writing inventories in ledgers, reading the 'Song of Solomon' at night,

So many verses before bed-time,

Because it was the Bible.

The dead fed you

Amid the slant stones of graveyards.

Pale ghosts who planted you

Came in the night-time

And let their thin hair blow through your clustered stems.

You are of the green sea,

And of the stone hills which reach a long distance.

You are of elm-shaded streets with little shops where they sell kites and marbles,

You are of great parks where everyone walks and nobody is at home.

You cover the blind sides of greenhouses

And lean over the top to say a hurry-word through the glass

To your friends, the grapes, inside.

Lilacs,

False blue,

White,

Purple,

Colour of lilac,

You have forgotten your Eastern origin,

The veiled women with eyes like panthers,

The swollen, aggressive turbans of jewelled Pashas.

Now you are a very decent flower,

A reticent flower,

A curiously clear-cut, candid flower,

Standing beside clean doorways,

Friendly to a house-cat and a pair of spectacles,

Making poetry out of a bit of moonlight

And a hundred or two sharp blossoms.

Maine knows you,

Has for years and years;

New Hampshire knows you,

And Massachusetts

And Vermont.

Cape Cod starts you along the beaches to Rhode Island;

Connecticut takes you from a river to the sea.

You are brighter than apples,

Sweeter than tulips,

You are the great flood of our souls

Bursting above the leaf-shapes of our hearts,

You are the smell of all Summers,

The love of wives and children,

The recollection of the gardens of little children,

You are State Houses and Charters

And the familiar treading of the foot to and fro on a road it knows.

May is lilac here in New England,

May is a thrush singing 'Sun up!' on a tip-top ash-tree,

May is white clouds behind pine-trees

Puffed out and marching upon a blue sky.

May is a green as no other,

May is much sun through small leaves,

May is soft earth,

And apple-blossoms,

And windows open to a South wind.

May is a full light wind of lilac

From Canada to Narragansett Bay.

Lilacs,

False blue,

White,

Purple,

Colour of lilac.

Heart-leaves of lilac all over New England,

Roots of lilac under all the soil of New England,

Lilac in me because I am New England,

Because my roots are in it,

Because my leaves are of it,

Because my flowers are for it,

Because it is my country

And I speak to it of itself

And sing of it with my own voice

Since certainly it is mine.

ROBERT FROST (1874-1963)

Another contender for the title of 'America's greatest poet', Robert Frost was deeply
influenced by the countryside of New England where he lived most of his life, although
his first collections of poems were published, with the encouragement of Rupert Brooke,
in England where he lived from 1912-1915. His portrayal of the natural world follows in
the footsteps of Wordsworth and Emerson, but has a style uniquely his own.
He also has the rare distinction of having been awarded three Pulitzer prizes.

THE ROAD NOT TAKEN

Two roads diverged in a yellow wood,
And sorry I could not travel both
And be one traveler, long I stood
And looked down one as far as I could
To where it bent in the undergrowth;

Then took the other, as just as fair,
And having perhaps the better claim,
Because it was grassy and wanted wear;
Though as for that, the passing there
Had worn them really about the same,

And both that morning equally lay
In leaves no step had trodden black.
Oh, I kept the first for another day!
Yet knowing how way leads on to way,
I doubted if I should ever come back.

I shall be telling this with a sigh
Somewhere ages and ages hence:
Two roads diverged in a wood, and I –
I took the one less traveled by,
And that has made all the difference.

STOPPING BY WOODS ON A SNOWY EVENING

Whose woods these are I think I know.
His house is in the village, though;
He will not see me stopping here
To watch his woods fill up with snow.

My little horse must think it queer
To stop without a farmhouse near
Between the woods and frozen lake
The darkest evening of the year.

He gives his harness bells a shake
To ask if there is some mistake.
The only other sound's the sweep
Of easy wind and downy flake.

The woods are lovely, dark and deep,
But I have promises to keep,
And miles to go before I sleep,
And miles to go before I sleep.

ACQUAINTED WITH THE NIGHT

I have been one acquainted with the night.
I have walked out in rain – and back in rain.
I have outwalked the furthest city light.

I have looked down the saddest city lane.
I have passed by the watchman on his beat
And dropped my eyes, unwilling to explain.

I have stood still and stopped the sound of feet
When far away an interrupted cry
Came over houses from another street,

But not to call me back or say goodbye;
And further still at an unearthly height,
One luminary clock against the sky
Proclaimed the time was neither wrong nor right.
I have been one acquainted with the night.

*The First World War inspired a whole generation of great writers who became
known as the 'War Poets'. It also killed most of them – Wilfred Owen within a week
of the Armistice in November 1918. The American Alan Seeger (see page 131)
lived for a while in Paris and volunteered to serve in the French
Foreign Legion. The works of these poets cover a gamut of emotions
from courage to despair, from bitterness to
a deep longing for home.*

EDWARD THOMAS (1878-1917)

ADLESTROP

Yes. I remember Adlestrop –
The name, because one afternoon
Of heat the express-train drew up there
Unwontedly. It was late June.

The steam hissed. Someone cleared his throat.
No one left and no one came
On the bare platform. What I saw
Was Adlestrop – only the name

And willows, willow-herb, and grass,
And meadowsweet, and haycocks dry,
No whit less still and lonely fair
Than the high cloudlets in the sky.

And for that minute a blackbird sang
Close by, and round him, mistier,
Farther and farther, all the birds
Of Oxfordshire and Gloucestershire.

SIEGFRIED SASSOON (1886-1967)

ATTACK

At dawn the ridge emerges massed and dun
In the wild purple of the glow'ring sun,
Smouldering through spouts of drifting smoke that shroud
The menacing scarred slope; and, one by one,
Tanks creep and topple forward to the wire.
The barrage roars and lifts. Then, clumsily bowed
With bombs and guns and shovels and battle-gear,
Men jostle and climb to meet the bristling fire.
Lines of grey, muttering faces, masked with fear,
They leave their trenches, going over the top,
While time ticks blank and busy on their wrists,
And hope, with furtive eyes and grappling fists,
Flounders in mud. O Jesus, make it stop!

RUPERT BROOKE (1887-1915)

THE SOLDIER

If I should die, think only this of me:
That there's some corner of a foreign field
That is for ever England. There shall be
In that rich earth a richer dust concealed;

OPPOSITE. THE BRIDGE BY HELEN ALLINGHAM

A dust whom England bore, shaped, made aware,

Gave, once, her flowers to love, her ways to roam,

A body of England's, breathing English air,

Washed by the rivers, blessed by suns of home.

And think, this heart, all evil shed away,

A pulse in the eternal mind, no less

Gives somewhere back the thoughts by England given;

Her sights and sounds; dreams happy as her day;

And laughter, learnt of friends; and gentleness,

In hearts at peace, under an English heaven.

THE OLD VICARAGE, GRANTCHESTER (extract)

(Anadyomene refers to a painting of Venus rising from the sea.)

Ah God! to see the branches stir

Across the moon at Grantchester!

To smell the thrilling-sweet and rotten

Unforgettable, unforgotten

River-smell and hear the breeze

Sobbing in the little trees.

Say, do the elm-clumps greatly stand

Still guardians of that holy land?

The chestnut shade, in reverend dream,

The yet unacademic stream?

Is dawn a secret shy and cold

Anadyomene, silver-gold?

And sunset still a golden sea

From Haslingfield to Madingley?

And after, ere the night is born,

Do hares come out about the corn?

Oh, is the water sweet and cool,

Gentle and brown, above the pool?

And laughs the immortal river still

Under the mill, under the mill?

Say, is there Beauty yet to find?

And Certainty? and Quiet kind?

Deep meadows yet, for to forget

The lies, and truths, and pain? . . . Oh! yet

Stands the Church clock at ten to three?

And is there honey still for tea?

ALAN SEEGER (1888-1916)

RENDEZVOUS

I have a rendezvous with Death

At some disputed barricade,

When Spring comes back with rustling shade

And apple-blossoms fill the air

I have a rendezvous with Death

When Spring brings back blue days and fair.

It may be he shall take my hand

And lead me into his dark land

And close my eyes and quench my breath

It may be I shall pass him still.

I have a rendezvous with Death

On some scarred slope of battered hill,

When Spring comes round again this year
And the first meadow-flowers appear.

God knows 'twere better to be deep
Pillowed in silk and scented down,
Where love throbs out in blissful sleep,
Pulse nigh to pulse, and breath to breath,
Where hushed awakenings are dear…
But I've a rendezvous with Death
At midnight in some flaming town,
When Spring trips north again this year,
And I to my pledged word am true,
I shall not fail that rendezvous.

WILFRED OWEN (1893-1918)

ANTHEM FOR DOOMED YOUTH

What passing-bells for these who die as cattle?
Only the monstrous anger of the guns.
Only the stuttering rifles' rapid battle
Can patter out their hasty orisons.
No mockeries for them from prayers or bells,
Nor any voice of mourning save the choirs, –
The shrill, demented choirs of wailing shells;
And bugles calling for them from sad shires.
What candles may be held to speed them all?
Not in the hands of boys, but in their eyes

Shall shine the holy glimmers of good-byes.

The pallor of girls' brows shall be their pall;

Their flowers the tenderness of silent minds,

And each slow dusk a drawing-down of blinds.

FUTILITY

Move him into the sun

Gently its touch awoke him once,

At home, whispering of fields unsown.

Always it woke him, even in France,

Until this morning and this snow.

If anything might rouse him now

The kind old sun will know.

Think how it wakes the seed –

Woke, once, the clays of a cold star.

Are limbs, so dear-achieved, are sides,

Full-nerved – still warm – too hard to stir?

Was it for this the clay grew tall?

– O what made fatuous sunbeams toil

To break earth's sleep at all?

D. H. LAWRENCE (1885-1930)

David Herbert Lawrence is best known for his novels, especially the controversial Lady

Chatterley's Lover, *but his poetry deserves to be more widely read. Much of it was*

written in the course of the broad-ranging travels which included Mexico and Australia,
as well as Germany and Italy and which occupied most of the last fifteen years of his life.

PIANO

Softly, in the dusk, a woman is singing to me;
Taking me back down the vista of years, till I see
A child sitting under the piano, in the boom of the tingling strings
And pressing the small, poised feet of a mother who smiles as she sings.

In spite of myself, the insidious mastery of song
Betrays me back, till the heart of me weeps to belong
To the old Sunday evenings at home, with winter outside
And hymns in the cosy parlour, the tinkling piano our guide.

So now it is vain for the singer to burst into clamour
With the great black piano appassionato. The glamour
Of childish days is upon me, my manhood is cast
Down in the flood of remembrance, I weep like a child for the past.

EZRA POUND (1885-1972)

Pound fell from popular esteem during the Second World War, when he espoused the
cause of Italian Fascism under Mussolini, and was responsible for anti-Semitic
broadcasts from Rome. Before that, however, he had been an influential advocate of
avant-garde poetry to whom Yeats, Eliot and Joyce all acknowledged a debt.

LONDON FOG BY ROSE BARTON

THE GARDEN

Like a skein of loose silk blown against a wall
She walks by the railing of a path in Kensington Gardens.
And she is dying piece-meal of a sort of emotional anaemia.

And round about there is a rabble
Of the filthy, sturdy, unkillable infants of the very poor.
They shall inherit the earth.

In her is the end of breeding.
Her boredom is exquisite and excessive.
She would like some one to speak to her,
And is almost afraid that I
will commit that indiscretion.

FRANCES CORNFORD (1886-1960)

Frances Cornford was the granddaughter of Charles Darwin and, confusingly, married the academic writer Francis Cornford. She is remembered primarily for this poem, whose opening lines are described in the Oxford Companion to English Literature *as 'curiously memorable though undistinguished'.*

TO A FAT LADY SEEN FROM THE TRAIN

O why do you walk through the fields in gloves,
Missing so much and so much?

O fat white woman whom nobody loves,

Why do you walk through the fields in gloves,

When the grass is soft as the breast of doves

And shivering-sweet to the touch?

O why do you walk through the fields in gloves,

Missing so much and so much?

T. S. ELIOT (1888-1965)

One of the great figures of twentieth-century English literature, American-born Thomas Stearns Eliot is now a household name the world over because he wrote a certain collection of poems about cats. He settled in England in 1914 and subsequently became a British subject and a member of the Church of England, though he later described himself as an Anglo-Catholic. The development of his religious beliefs is charted by his later poetry. As a director of the publishers Faber & Faber he had a significant influence on the development of a whole generation of poets, including Auden and Spender. He was also an important critic and playwright, his most successful plays being Murder in the Cathedral *(about Thomas à Becket) and the comedy* The Cocktail Party.

THE LOVE SONG OF J. ALFRED PRUFROCK (extract)

Let us go then, you and I,

When the evening is spread out against the sky

Like a patient etherised upon a table;

Let us go, through certain half-deserted streets,

The muttering retreats

Of restless nights in one-night cheap hotels

And sawdust restaurants with oyster-shells:
Streets that follow like a tedious argument
Of insidious intent
To lead you to an overwhelming question . . .
Oh, do not ask, 'What is it?'
Let us go and make our visit.

In the room the women come and go
Talking of Michelangelo.

The yellow fog that rubs its back upon the window-panes,
The yellow smoke that rubs its muzzle on the window-panes
Licked its tongue into the corners of the evening,
Lingered upon the pools that stand in drains,
Let fall upon its back the soot that falls from chimneys,
Slipped by the terrace, made a sudden leap,
And seeing that it was a soft October night,
Curled once about the house, and fell asleep.

And indeed there will be time
For the yellow smoke that slides along the street
Rubbing its back upon the window-panes;
There will be time, there will be time
To prepare a face to meet the faces that you meet;
There will be time to murder and create,
And time for all the works and days of hands
That lift and drop a question on your plate;
Time for you and time for me,
And time yet for a hundred indecisions,
And for a hundred visions and revisions,
Before the taking of a toast and tea.

In the room the women come and go
Talking of Michelangelo.

And indeed there will be time
To wonder, 'Do I dare?' and, 'Do I dare?'
Time to turn back and descend the stair,
With a bald spot in the middle of my hair –
(They will say: 'How his hair is growing thin!')
My morning coat, my collar mounting firmly to the chin,
My necktie rich and modest, but asserted by a simple pin –
(They will say: 'But how his arms and legs are thin!')
Do I dare
Disturb the universe?
In a minute there is time
For decisions and revisions which a minute will reverse.

For I have known them all already, known them all –
Have known the evenings, mornings, afternoons,
I have measured out my life with coffee spoons;
I know the voices dying with a dying fall
Beneath the music from a farther room.
So how should I presume ?

And I have known the eyes already, known them all –
The eyes that fix you in a formulated phrase,
And when I am formulated, sprawling on a pin,
When I am pinned and wriggling on the wall,
Then how should I begin
To spit out all the butt-ends of my days and ways?
And how should I presume?

And I have known the arms already, known them all –
Arms that are braceleted and white and bare
(But in the lamplight, downed with light brown hair!)
Is it perfume from a dress
That makes me so digress?
Arms that lie along a table, or wrap about a shawl.
And should I then presume?
And how should I begin?

THE WASTE LAND

1. THE BURIAL OF THE DEAD (extract)

April is the cruellest month, breeding
Lilacs out of the dead land, mixing
Memory and desire, stirring
Dull roots with spring rain.
Winter kept us warm, covering
Earth in forgetful snow, feeding
A little life with dried tubers.
Summer surprised us, coming over the Starnbergersee
With a shower of rain; we stopped in the colonnade,
And went on in sunlight, into the Hofgarten,
And drank coffee, and talked for an hour.
Bin gar keine Russin, stamm' aus Litauen, echt deutsch.
And when we were children, staying at the arch-duke's,
My cousin's, he took me out on a sled,
And I was frightened. He said, Marie,
Marie, hold on tight. And down we went.

In the mountains, there you feel free.

I read, much of the night, and go south in the winter.

❧❧

JOHN BETJEMAN (1906-1984)

One of England's best-loved poets, John Betjeman owes his popularity to the sheer readability of his work and to the genial personality that became well known through radio and television. He was a passionate admirer of English architecture, particularly church architecture, and this famous poem is a rant against the mediocrity that he saw taking over the country he adored.

SLOUGH

Come, friendly bombs, and fall on Slough

It isn't fit for humans now,

There isn't grass to graze a cow

Swarm over, Death!

Come, bombs, and blow to smithereens

Those air-conditioned, bright canteens,

Tinned fruit, tinned meat, tinned milk, tinned beans

Tinned minds, tinned breath.

Mess up the mess they call a town –

A house for ninety-seven down

And once a week a half-a-crown
For twenty years,

And get that man with double chin
Who'll always cheat and always win,
Who washes his repulsive skin
In women's tears,

And smash his desk of polished oak
And smash his hands so used to stroke
And stop his boring dirty joke
And make him yell.

But spare the bald young clerks who add
The profits of the stinking cad;
It's not their fault that they are mad,
They've tasted Hell.

It's not their fault they do not know
The birdsong from the radio,
It's not their fault they often go
To Maidenhead

And talk of sports and makes of cars
In various bogus Tudor bars
And daren't look up and see the stars
But belch instead.

In labour-saving homes, with care
Their wives frizz out peroxide hair

And dry it in synthetic air
And paint their nails.

Come, friendly bombs, and fall on Slough
To get it ready for the plough.
The cabbages are coming now;
The earth exhales.

W. H. AUDEN (1907-1973)

Another twentieth-century giant, Auden was a protégé of T. S. Eliot, a friend of Stephen Spender and Louis MacNeice and a profound influence on almost every poet who came after him. This poem, read at the funeral in the film Four Weddings and a Funeral, *brought his work almost overnight to the attention of an immeasurably wider audience.*

TWELVE SONGS (extract)

Stop all the clocks, cut off the telephone,
Prevent the dog from barking with a juicy bone,
Silence the pianos and with muffled drum
Bring out the coffin, let the mourners come.

Let aeroplanes circle moaning overhead
Scribbling on the sky the message He Is Dead,
Put the crepe bows round the white necks of the public doves,
Let the traffic policemen wear black cotton gloves.

He was my North, my South, my East and West,

My working week and my Sunday's rest,

My noon, my midnight, my talk, my song,

I thought that love would last for ever: I was wrong.

The stars are not wanted now: put out every one;

Pack up the moon and dismantle the sun;

Pour away the ocean and sweep up the wood.

For nothing now can ever come to any good.

LOUIS MACNEICE (1907-1963)

A friend of Auden and Stephen Spender, Belfast-born MacNeice was educated
in England and worked as a writer/producer for the BBC, where he earned
acclaim for his radio plays which has at times overshadowed his
reputation as a poet. His simple but impeccable choice of words and the
unusual half-rhymes that characterise his poetry
give it an enduring appeal.

SNOW

The room was suddenly rich and the great bay-window was

Spawning snow and pink roses against it

Soundlessly collateral and incompatible:

World is suddener than we fancy it.

World is crazier and more of it than we think,

Incorrigibly plural. I peel and portion

A tangerine and spit the pips and feel

The drunkenness of things being various.

And the fire flames with a bubbling sound for world

Is more spiteful and gay than one supposes –

On the tongue on the eyes on the ears in the palms of one's hands –

There is more than glass between the snow and the huge roses.

DYLAN THOMAS (1914-1953)

Wales's greatest poet of the twentieth century spoke no Welsh and left his native land at the age of twenty to live in London and to travel frequently to the United States. His greatest work, Under Milk Wood, *was originally a radio play and was subsequently adapted into a play and a film. Sadly, Thomas succumbed to alcoholism before he was able to enjoy the fruits of this success.*

DO NOT GO GENTLE INTO THAT GOOD NIGHT

Do not go gentle into that good night,

Old age should burn and rave at close of day;

Rage, rage against the dying of the light.

Though wise men at their end know dark is right,

Because their words had forked no lightning they

Do not go gentle into that good night.

Good men, the last wave by, crying how bright
Their frail deeds might have danced in a green bay,
Rage, rage against the dying of the light.

Wild men who caught and sang the sun in flight,
And learn, too late, they grieved it on its way,
Do not go gentle into that good night.

Grave men, near death, who see with blinding sight
Blind eyes could blaze like meteors and be gay,
Rage, rage against the dying of the light.

And you, my father, there on the sad height,
Curse, bless, me now with your fierce tears, I pray.
Do not go gentle into that good night.
Rage, rage against the dying of the light.

TED HUGHES (1930-1998)

*The notoriety surrounding Ted Hughes' unhappy marriage to the American
poet Sylvia Plath has somewhat overshadowed his undoubted genius.
His poetry, which frequently depict both the beauty and the violence of
the natural world, has been described as brutal, but he had the gift of bringing
seemingly banal subjects (such as tractors and thistles) to memorable life.
He became Poet Laureate in 1984, on the death of John Betjeman.*

OPPOSITE. WELSH LANDSCAPE

TRACTOR

The tractor stands frozen – an agony
To think of. All night
Snow packed its open entrails. Now a head-pincering gale,
A spill of molten ice, smoking snow,
Pours into its steel.
At white heat of numbness it stands
In the aimed hosing of ground-level fieriness.

It defies flesh and won't start.
Hands are like wounds already
Inside armour gloves, and feet are unbelievable
As if the toe-nails were all just torn off.
I stare at it in hatred. Beyond it
The copse hisses – capitulates miserably
In the fleeing, failing light. Starlings,
A dirtier sleetier snow, blow smokily, unendingly, over
Towards plantations eastward.
All the time the tractor is sinking
Through the degrees, deepening
Into its hell of ice.

The starter lever
Cracks its action, like a snapping knuckle.
The battery is alive – but like a lamb
Trying to nudge its solid-frozen mother
While the seat claims my buttock-bones, bites
With the space-cold of earth, which it has joined
In one solid lump.

I squirt commercial sure-fire

Down the black throat – it just coughs.

It ridicules me – a trap of iron stupidity

I've stepped into. I drive the battery

As if I were hammering and hammering

The frozen arrangement to pieces with a hammer

And it jabbers laughing pain-crying mockingly

Into happy life.

And stands

Shuddering itself full of heat, seeming to enlarge slowly

Like a demon demonstrating

A more-than-usually-complete materialization

Suddenly it jerks from its solidarity

With the concrete, then lurches towards a stanchion

Bursting with superhuman well-being and abandon

Shouting Where Where?

Worse iron is waiting. Power-lift kneels,

Levers awake imprisoned deadweight,

Shackle-pins bedded in cast-iron cow-shit.

The blind and vibrating condemned obedience

Of iron to the cruelty of iron,

Wheels screeched out of their night-locks –

Fingers

Among the tormented

Tonnage and burning of iron

Eyes
Weeping in the wind of chloroform

And the tractor, streaming with sweat,
Raging and trembling and rejoicing.

THISTLES

Against the rubber tongues of cows and the hoeing hands of men
Thistles spike the summer air
And crackle open under a blue-black pressure.

Everyone a revengeful burst
Of resurrection, a grasped fistful
Of splintered weapons and Icelandic frost thrust up

From the underground stain of a decayed Viking,
They are like pale hair and the gutturals of dialects.
Every one manages a plume of blood.

Then they grow grey like men.
Mown down, it is a feud. Their sons appear
Stiff with weapons, fighting back over the same ground.

꽃

SEAMUS HEANEY (1939–)

Born and educated in Northern Ireland, Seamus Heaney moved to the Republic in 1972 and has made his home there ever since. He also occupies a Chair of Poetry at Oxford. Probably the greatest living Irish poet, his work is strongly influenced by the countryside of his childhood and the political background against which he grew up.

SUNLIGHT

There was a sunlit absence.
The helmeted pump in the yard
heated its iron,
water honeyed

in the slung bucket
and the sun stood
like a griddle cooling
against the wall

of each long afternoon.
So, her hands scuffled
over the bakeboard,
the reddening stove

sent its plaque of heat
against her where she stood
in a floury apron
by the window.

Now she dusts the board

with a goose's wing,

now sits, broad lapped,

with whitened nails

and measling shins:

here is a space again,

the scone rising to the tick of two clocks.

And here is love

like a tinsmith's scoop

sunk past its gleam

in the meal-bin.

❧

OPPOSITE. ELDERLY COUNTRY COUPLE

Index of First Lines

I have a rendezvous with Death 131
I have been one acquainted with the night 126
I met a traveller from an antique land 72
I remember, I remember 80
I tell you, hopeless grief is passionless 104
I wandered lonely as a cloud 52
I will arise and go now, and go to Innisfree 119
If I should die, think only this of me 128
If the red slayer thinks he slays 86
If you can keep your head when all about you 117
In a somer seson whan soft was the sunne 14
In Xanadu did Kubla Khan 58
It is a ancient Mariner 54

Januar: By this fire I warme my handis 18

Know then thyself, presume not God to scan 36

Let us go then, you and I 137
Lilacs 120
Like a skein of loose silk blown against a wall 135

'Mine and yours 84
Move him into the sun 133
Much have I travelled in the realms of gold 77
My life closed twice before its close 111

Nothing is so beautiful as spring – 112

O Captain! my Captain! our fearful trip is done 94
O say, can you see, by the dawn's early light 63
O to be in England 105
O why do you walk through the fields in gloves 136
O Wild West Wind, thou breath of Autumn's being 74
On either side the river lie 97

Peruse my leaves thro' ev'ry part 34

Season of mists and mellow fruitfulness 78
Should auld acquaintance be forgot 51
Softly, in the dusk, a woman is singing to me 134
Stop all the clocks, cut off the telephone 143

Acknowledgements

'If' by **Rudyard Kipling** by permission of A.P. Watt Ltd on behalf of the The National Trust for Places of Historical Interest or Natural Beauty. 'Twelve songs IX' by **W.H. Auden** from *Collected Poems* by W.H. Auden, copyright 1937 and renewed 1965 by W.H. Auden, reprinted by permission of Faber and Faber Ltd and of Random House, Inc. 'Slough' from *Collected Poems* by **John Betjeman**, reprinted by permission of John Murray (Publishers) Ltd. 'To a Fat Lady seen from the Train' by **Frances Cornford,** from *Frances Cornford: Collected Poems*, published by Cresset Press. Reprinted by permission of The Random House Group Ltd.'The Love Song of J Alfred Prufrock' (extract) and 'The Waste Land' (extract) from *Collected Poems 1909-1962* by **T.S. Eliot**, reprinted by permission of the Publishers, Faber and Faber Ltd and of Harcourt and Company,Inc. 'The Road not Taken' by **Robert Frost** from *The Poetry of Robert Frost, edited by Edward Connery Lathem,* by permission of The Estate of Robert Frost and Jonathan Cape as publisher. Used by permission of The Random House Group Limited. *The Poetry of Robert Frost, edited by Edward Connery Lathem* Copyright 1944 by Robert Frost, © 1969 by Henry Holt and Company. Reprinted by permission of Henry Holt and Company, LLC. 'Sunlight' by **Seamus Heaney** from *Opened Ground: Selected Poems 1966–1996*. Copyright © 1998 by Seamus Heaney. Reprinted by permission of the Publishers, Faber and Faber Ltd and of Farrar Straus and Giroux, LLC. 'Tractor' from *Moortown* and 'Thistles' from *Wodwo* by **Ted Hughes**, reprinted by permission of the Publishers, Faber and Faber Ltd. 'Snow' by **Louis MacNeice** from *Collected Poems by Louis MacNeice*, published by Faber and Faber Ltd, by permission of David Higham Associates. 'The Garden' from *Collected Shorter Poems* by **Ezra Pound**, reprinted by permission of the Publishers, Faber and Faber Ltd. Ezra Pound, from *Personae*, copyright © 1926 by Ezra Pound. Reprinted by permission of New Directions Publishing Corp. 'Attack' by **Siegfried Sassoon**, copyright Siegfried Sassoon by kind permission of George Sassoon and of Viking Penguin, a division of Penguin Putnam Inc. "Attack", from Collected Poems of Siegfried Sassoon by Siegfried Sassoon, copyright 1918, 1920 by E.P. Dutton. Copyright 1936, 1946, 1947, 1948 by Siegfried Sassoon. .'Do not go gentle into that good night' from **Dylan Thomas** from *Collected Poems by Dylan Thomas*, published by J M Dent.Reprinted by permission of David Higham Associates. 'The Lake Isle of Innisfree' by **W.B. Yeats**, by permission of A.P. Watt Ltd on behalf of Michael B Yeats and of Scribner, a Division of Simon & Schuster, Inc.from *The Collected Poems of W.B. Yeats*, Revised Second Edition edited by Richard J. Finneran (New York: Scribner, 1996).

Although every effort has been made to trace the copyright holders. The editor apologizes for any omission which may have occurred.